Why Every Man Should Read The Bible From Cover-To-Cover At Least Once

By

Pamela M. Harris

First Edition
First Printing 200 Oct. 2002

Library of Congress Control Number: 2003090247

ISBN: 978-1-57502-222-2

Additional copies may be obtained by sending a
check or money order for $12.95 to the address below.

Attn: Pamela M. Harris
P.O. Box 403
Riverside, NJ 08075

Printed in the United States by Morris Publishing®
Kearney, Nebraska

Dedication

This book is dedicated to Janice Goddelle, who was the first person to encourage me to read the Bible from cover-to-cover; my precious children, Brandie and Reginald, who patiently tolerated me; To my darling "twin" brother, Jimmy, who I kept in mind as I wrote; and to Shirelle, who allowed me to call her at odd hours of the night with questions.

My very special thanks go to my big brother, Tony, for his encouraging words and prayers over the telephone, at the most needed hours; and to Joanne Caprice---who WAS a stranger that had compassion for me, and helped me see this project to completion!

Most important, I give praise and deep thanks to God, my Heavenly Father, who made all of this possible.

TABLE OF CONTENTS

A WORD TO THE READER

Since July 1989, I've engaged in market research. I've conducted pharmaceutical studies to help pharmacists decide whether or not to put a particular medicine on the market. I've done consumer surveys to test new product concepts and television commercials' effectiveness. I've studied the elderly to try to understand the linkage between their lifestyles and lifespans. I've worked intimately with drug abusers to study why their rehabilitation programs have failed them. And I've studied teenagers to better understand the problems of teenage pregnancies.

In essence, I've engaged in well over 100 different studies--all designed to help business owners make lucrative decisions, or to help U.S. Government agencies enhance the overall effectiveness of their social programs. In all of these personally rewarding experiences, I've remained objective and professional, NEVER offering my opinions. Instead, I was a good listener, and I restricted myself to collecting opinions.

About May 1995, I stumbled over some independent voluntary research: The Word of God! I began reading the Holy Bible from cover-to-cover until December 1995. I was blown away by the wealth of information in it. I learned everything I needed to know about life. I was amazed at how drastically different God's Word was from what others had lead me to believe throughout my life. I grew spiritually, mentally, and emotionally, and I haven't been the same since!

Because I have a passion for research and I love passing along useful information to the public, I broke a record in my career and did something I've NEVER done before!! I was so awestruck by the Holy Bible that I found it irresistable to be objective and hold my tongue. I OFFERED MY OPINIONS!! This is a big, "No-No" in the market research industry. Yet I was helpless. I would have exploded if I didn't write this book, **Why Every Man Should Read The Bible From Cover-To-Cover, At Least Once**.

So, if I am offensive, please forgive me. But my intent is to present you with the facts that I've gathered from the Bible, and offer you my deepest opinion: you should read the treasures of the Holy Bible for yourself.

i

SIGNIFICANCE OF MY POSITION

Why do I tell you about my position as a market researcher? I hope that you can see me, the author, as a researcher who's gathered information from the Word of God. But more importantly, I hope that you can see yourself as my client. Then, as every client does, you will make decisions based on the data that I provide you with.

Since you are a decision-maker and you have this powerful position--after you have read this book, YOU WILL DECIDE: (1)Whether or not to read the Bible from cover-to-cover; (2) Whether or not to accept Jesus Christ as your Personal Savior and live for Christ's sake; and (3) Whether or not you want to experience life and joy or sadness and death.

I am honored by my position and I cheer you on in your powerful position as my client. May God Bless you in your decision-making.

YOUR STATE OF MIND AS YOU READ

Before you begin reading this book, it's necessary for you to recognize that there are two types of readers. There are several reasons why this distinction is important. The whole purpose of this book is to inspire you to read the Bible from cover-to-cover. However, there's a particular reader that I have in mind (although my prayer is that EVERYONE will read it.) Thus, the purpose of explaining the two different types of readers is to help you understand the reader that I had in mind when I wrote this book; to help you assess the type of reader that you are; and finally, to present you with what you can expect to gain from following my advice.

There are two types of readers that we'll call the **Reluctant Reader** and the **Enthusiastic Reader**. The reluctant reader, at an early age, was constantly reminded, and maybe even forcefully told, "You NEED to read!" This reader read out of obedience. But with the obedience came the frustration, annoyance, and even a sought of sulky giving-in. Unfortunately, this reader adapted a style of learning in anger, arguing and fighting with words given, and looking for mistakes throughout the books they were "forced" to read! In essence, the reluctant reader is less likely to get the ultimate experience from a book, such as the Holy Bible.

However, the enthusiastic reader loves reading, loves learning, loves growing, and loves truth. As a result, they will embrace books such as the Holy Bible. They are eager, to gain ALL that this Book has to offer: Love, growth, wisdom, truth, guidance, comfort, and Joy!

Again, I express my prayers that each person who receives this book is inspired, motivated, and blessed with all their needs. But I'm failing at my job again, as a researcher. I'm being bias, because in all due respect, this book is for spiritually ill, sad, lost, and/or lonely readers WHO ARE HUNGRY for truth, love, growth, guidance, comfort and joy! Those of you who fit this description are my targeted audience. Still, blessings upon you all.

INTRODUCTION

There were people in my household who just couldn't seem to grasp or understand why I was so consumed with reading the Holy Bible! At times, they even got annoyed, questioning, "What's with all this Bible reading anyway?"

I explained myself in bits and pieces as best I could. But the bottom line was that after I got through the first (3) books---Genesis, Exodus, and Leviticus, I was hooked! I couldn't stop reading!

In the beginning of the Bible, I got a complete, detailed picture of who God was; what God had done; and how He did it. God created the universe and He did it by speaking WORDS. As I read each day, I gained so much understanding about the nature of man and God. By the time I got to the New Testament, I learned how to live. Finally, I got specific instructions for my present and future life. By the time I read the Bible from cover-to-cover, I knew one thing: There's POWER in GOD'S WORD.

So as we proceed into this book, expect for several things to come to you. First, expect a definition of what it is that I am encouraging you to read. Learn about the vast variety that are available to you, and how to choose the ONE that's BEST for you. After you learn the technical definition of God's Word, I will give you (7) reasons why you should read the Bible from cover-to-cover, at least once.

Then, I can't resist giving you a personal testimony on all the many things the Bible did for me. I hope that through my testimony you will see the emphasis on the unrelinquishing fact that the Bible has changed my life forever.

Finally, I will share with you all that I have learned from each book in the Bible. I share my knowledge with you in deep hopes that you will NOT merely take my words for truth, but you will experience the words for yourself. Not only will you experience the reading of the Bible, but I believe you will witness changes occuring in your life. You will feel real joy for the first time in life!

My recommendation, with love, is that each day at 6:00 A.M. or 9:00 P.M. or whatever is your favorite time of day, you kick up your heels, relax with a glass of warm or cold milk and honey, and read for AT LEAST 30 minutes. When you have fed your body God's Word from cover-to-cover, you will say, "Wow! I feel like a new person." You will smile from this nourishment, and my heart will be pleased at all of your smiling faces. So, be blessed in the Name of Jesus.

MORE THAN A WORK OF ART

According to the Bible study teachings under Pastor Frederick C. Johnson of Second Baptist Church, the Library of Congress has over 22 million books in it's possession, and 30,000 new title releases annually. Yet, the Bible stands as the All-time best seller, distributing 100 million copies worldwide annually.

The Bible is a unique, miraculous, amazing collaboration of prose, poetry, romance, mystery, biography, science and HISTORY. There are some 774,746 words covering EVERY subject you could imagine. Why is this book so amazing? The Bible had no editor or publishing house to oversee its 50 different authors, living in 10 different countries over a 1,600-year span. Yet, it's all ONE story! For example, the Book of Genesis is ultimately fulfilled in the Book of Revelation, when in Genesis 1, God creates the heavens and the earth. Then, in Revelations 21, God created the new heavens and earth. From cover-to-cover, the Bible presents a consistent picture of ONE TRUE GOD, ONE cause of man's troubles (Sin), and ONE universal solution (Jesus Christ, God's Son). Still, the greatest miracle of the Bible is that everything in it has been verified by archaeologists and historians. This includes the Walls of Jericho, and the existence of Ponte Pontius, who plotted the death of Jesus Christ! In essence, ONLY God could have inspired a book of such unity, consistency, depths, and lacking unsolvable contradictions.

ORIGIN OF THE OLD TESTAMENT

There's a very long, detailed history of the development of the many books that we know as the Bible. However, as this is NOT a book on the history of the Bible, I will NOT present you with such details. Instead, I will explain to you what happened to the original text; what happened after the destruction of the original text; the origin of the Masoretic text and the King James version; and how accuracy was checked.

As explained by teacher and Pastor, Frederick C. Johnson, we do not have any of the original manuscripts that any of the apostles or prophets wrote. These original writings were either lost or degraded in time because of the material they were written on. These materials were written on papyrus, a specially dried leaf for purposes of writing on. However, in time, this material dried out and crumbled. Weather and mold or fungus were also contributing factors to the deterioration of original manuscripts. In addition to these factors, there were no printing presses; and during the second and third century A.D., there were many attempts to destroy the Bible or its individual writings, by way of tribulations and burnings. Thus, these were the obstacles involved in the preserving and distribution of the Bible.

Despite these obstacles, the Bible has stood the test of times. So, the magic question is "how?" Again, without engaging in a deep, historical search, we will look at HOW the Bible has endured until today. First, the Bible from the writings of the Law of Moses is considered the Words of God, given on Mount Sinai. From a historical standpoint, whoever disobeyed the Words of Moses, also referred to as the Laws of God, were stricken with sickness and disease. It was these Laws which became sacred, and thus passed from generation to generation, as commanded by God.

Although we don't have the original words written by Moses, centuries after Moses, two famous kings of Israel found the Law of Moses in the Ark of the Covenant. This resulted in a great revival.

The Dead Sea Scrolls, found in the caves of Qumram, dated 800 to 1000 years earlier than they were found, resulted in the formation of the Masoretic text, which led to early translations of the (OT) Old Testament, including the King James Version.

Before the KJV, how were these scriptures preserved? Jewish scribes carefully copied the Words of God from original OT scriptures and verified their accuracy by counting the numbers of letters per page and the number of words per page with a middle count mark to denote the letter of the original page. So, say for example there were 1,000 letters per page and the center letter was 500. The letter at the 500 mark on both the copy and the original had to be the same. This very meticulous, fanatical way of verifying accuracy of the scriptures, is how the entire OT was preserved from year-to-year.

Although this is an extremely brief overview of how the OT was formed and translated from Hebrew into Greek, and into the Authorized Version of King James, the most critical point here is that the Bible has a historically documented beginning, and great care was given to keep God's Word as accurate as humanly possible.

What, then, is the significance to all of this? In 1644, King James had the Bible translated under his authority for common distribution at a time when the Bible was highly respected and revered. Today, the Bible is a magical, marvelous Book that teaches you wisdom, encouragement and instructions for life here on earth and thereafter. In conclusion, the Bible is a Book of Truth and a way of Life.

Consider the fact that the Gospel has been translated into over one thousand languages, and the Bible is distributed in millions of copies throughout the world annually. Then look at the chronology of the making of the Bible on the following pages. Finally, decide for yourself. Is the Bible NOT Living Waters? Is there NOT magic or miracle and power in the Word of God?!

CHRONOLOGY OF THE BIBLE

Passover and Exodus......Stories of Abraham, Isaac, Jacob. 1750 B.C.
Ten Commandments given to Moses on Mt. Sinai
Books of the Kings.................................
Stories of the Conquest of Palestine.....Old Testament translated into
Greek 250-50 B.C.
Prophets...
Psalms...

Letters and Gospels in Greek written on Papyrus 50-100 A.D.
Dead Sea Scrolls (Old Testament manuscripts) ?150 A.D.
Greek Codex Sinaiticus (earliest complete copy of NT about 350 A.D.
Bible Translated into Latin by St. Jerome - i.e. The Vulgate 400A.D.
Scribes copying manuscripts on parchment
Wyclif Version (Bible translated into English) 1382
Wyclif Version (later) 1395 - 1408
Printing Press invented about 1450 A.D.

The Vulgate was printed by Gutenberg about 1456 A.D. This Bible
before printing was distributed over 1,000 years prior, in Euroup.
These handwritten copies, completed in year 404, came from Hebrew
and Greek originals. This is the First Bible to be printed, in Mainz
Germany. Today, only about 40 copies exist, and they're worth about
$400,000.

Greek-Latin Bible published by Erasmus 1466 - 1536 A.D.
Wyclif Version in Scots (Nisbet) 1520
Tyndale Version 1525
Coverdale Version 1535
Matthew Version 1537
Geneva Bible 1560
Bishops' Bible 1568
Rhemish New Testament 1582
Douay Bible in English 1582 - 1610 A.D.
King James Version - 1611
King James Version - Present-Day Wording
Mr. Whiston's Primative New Testament 1745
The New Testament with an Analysis (John Wesley) 1790
The Holy Bible - Translated from the Greek. 1808
The Sacred Writings of the Apostles and Evangelists of Jesus
Christ, Commonly styled after the New Testament. Campbell
MacKnight and Doddridge 1826
The Holy Bible - Translated According to the Letter and Idiom of
the Original Languages (Robert Young) 1862
Revised Version 1881
The Twentieth Century New Testament (1st Edition) 1898-1901
American Standard Version 1901
The New Testament in Modern Speech (Weymouth) 1903

The Twentieth Century New Testament (Revised Edition) 1904

The Corrected English New Testament (Lloyd) 1905

The Modern Reader's Bible (Moulton) 1907

The New Testament, An American Translation (Goodspeed) 1923

The Centenary Translation of the New Testament (Helen Montgomery) 1924

The People's New Covenant (New Testament) Scriptural Writings, (Overbury) 1925

Concordant Version of the Sacred Scriptures, "New Testament," An Idiomatic, Consistent, Emphasized Version. (Concordant Publishing Concern, Los Angeles) 1926

A New Translation of the Bible (Moffatt, Final Edition) 1935.

The New Testament According to the Eastern Text Translated From Original Aramaic Sources (George M. Lamsa) 1940

The New Testament in Basic English 1941

The New Testament Translated From The Latin Vulgate (Confraternity Revision of the Challoner-Rheims Version) 1941

The Holy Scriptures Containing The Old and New Testament. An Inspired Revision of the Authorized Version (Joseph Smith, Jr.) A New Corrected Edition, 1944

The New Testament in the Translation of Monsignor Ronald Knox 1944.

Berkeley Version of the New Testament From the Original Greek with Brief Footnotes (Gerrit Verkuyl) 1945.

Revised Standard Version, 1946.

New World Translation of the Christian Greek Scriptures, Rendered From The Original Language By the New World Bible Translation Committee, (Watchtower Bible & Tract Society) 1950

The New Testament. A Translation In The Language of the People (Charles B. Williams) 1950.

The New Testament, A New Translation in Plain English (C.K. Williams) 1952.

Catholic Confraternity Bible 1952

American Revised Standard Version 1952

The New Testament in Modern English (J.B. Phillips) 1958

New English Bible - New Testament 1961.

The Living Bible (Paraphased) A Thought-for-Thought Translation (Tyndale) 1971.

PROBLEMS FACING THE BIBLE

The Bible has a history of over 4,000 years that's been documented by archaeologists' findings, death records, and genealogy records found in Europe today, that trace all the way back to the birth of Jesus Christ. It is a consistent compilation of 52 Books into One Book inspired by God; and it is one of the most widely referenced books in the world. For example, out of (50) different religions and cults, they have each taken some foundational truth from the Bible to form their own religions.

Even though the Bible is a wonderful Book of Life and a Book of Truth, it still faces several critical problems. A major problem facing the Bible today is that God's Word has been so devalued by man--- that scientists, scholars, philosophers, and other social "elites" are trivializing it to a book of myths, fables, and fairy tales. The result of these men's lack of wisdom is an influencing of the public to also believe that the Bible is NOT based on truth. The problem with a widespread population of nonbelievers, who devalue the Word of God is chaos, senseless murders, increasing drug wars, and massive stealing, starting with ghetto thieves and corporate crooks, right on to government swindlers and embezzlers.

This chaos is attributed to man devaluing the Word of God, because God's Word clearly speaks against all of these evils. But more than that, the Bible instructs you on how to experience peace and joy, and how to live. So, in essence, man has created a system or way of life that's totally contrary to the Word of God, calling God's Word folly, and replacing it with a system that's failing every day.

Another problem facing the Bible today is man trying to capitalize on it for personal gain. For example, man has totally denounced the King James Version, calling it inaccurate, inconsistent, and totally unclear. Yet, the King James Version was translated in an era when the Word of God was highly respected; and the 32 different translations available today, were largely translated in an era of capitalism. Money, money, and more money. In addition, the King James Version is the only translation that no one has copyrights to, and therefore cannot capitalize on it. But, perhaps it's a coincidence that no one can make money off of the KJV and at the same time, it just HAPPENS to be the most denounced, controversial Bible on the market today.

Still, there are several problems with some of the translated versions of the Bible. First, many translators are not even certain of the deity of God, the Father and His Son, Jesus Christ. Their objective is to water down the gospel into easy-to-understand language. Accuracy is not nearly as much of a priority as easy-to-understand language that will, in return, generate increased sales. Sadly, the ultimate goal is to make money.

In addition, when there's 32 different translations of the Bible, and as many as 12 different interpretations of a single Scripture, the result is confusion and discouragement! Let's give a hypothetical example of five men and women gathering for a home Bible Study. They each have their particular translated version.

They could easily become bewildered when they discover, "Well my Bible says this," and someone else says, "well, my Bible says that."

If they're a group of truth seekers, and they're not under any leader-ship or guidance, and they're babies in Christ---Satan, through man, has certainly set up an occasion for debates, arguments, confusion, and discouragement for determining, "What is the Truth?"

The problem with the Bible is that God's Word is so awesome, powerful, and filled with truth; and MAN, in general, DOESN'T LIKE THE TRUTH! For example, man is generally self-righteous, self-cen-tered and egotistical. And the last thing he wants to hear is that he's born evil in nature and has to be taught to be good; that he is NOTH-ING WITHOUT GOD and EVERYTHING through Christ Jesus! Man wants to believe that he has ultimate control over his life; he's good in nature; and God should "serve" or bless him for his "goodness." It can be the hardest lesson in life, to forsake self, and live for Jesus, and rely solely on God! This stomps out self-sufficiency, self-gratification, and the ego.

When you don't like the truth, you try to distort it, compromise with it, cling to some of it and reject the rest, learn all of it for the sake of knowledge, but apply none of it to your life. You do everything, but truely accept it and make it your way of life.

As you can see from the history of the Bible, because of this problem, man has consistently tampered with God's Word. While some men held onto God's Word, others tried to translate it into easy-to-understand language. Others held onto the Old Testament, or denounced the Old Testament and held onto the New Testament. Then some used bits and pieces of the Old and New, to create their own truths. If you decide to further investigate these translations by referring to the Bibliography, you will discover that SEVERAL of the translators have MYSTERIOUSLY lost their ability to speak! If you must have a Bible Version other than the King James Version, I strongly urge you to do a little research on the Translations on the market today! The information you discover will astound you.

As you will see in the following chart, some translators just watered down God's Word to what they called "easy-to-understand" language. They used fewer words to create "modern" versions, such as Weymouth, Moffatt, and Goodspeed. Unfortunatley, really important words were sometimes lost!

BOOK/CHAPTER	KJV	American Standard Version - ASV	Revised Standard Version - RSV
Matthew 5	1081	1056	1002
Mark 1 & 2	1654	1618	1534
Luke 8	1431	1431	1367
Romans 8	904	898	898

WHAT DOES THIS MEAN?

Because there are so many Bible translations on the market today, and so many motives behind the different translations; and because man doesn't like the truth---it is necessary for you to be aware of the very things that can keep you from learning the truth. Once you are aware, then you are prepared to seek a Bible that is translated closest to the original majority text. If you are concerned about the complexity of the book, I suggest you obtain a King James Student Bible, to help you along as you read. Just remember that the commentaries include man's thoughts, and the Scriptures are God's Word. This means you can accept or reject man's thoughts, but you SHOULD ACCEPT ALL of God's Word. Remember also that God WANTS you to have the truth, and since there is power in prayers, you can simply get a King James Version and ask God to illuminate to you wherever you need understanding. Finally, remember that you will NOT get EVERYTHING the Bible has to offer in a single reading. You are simply feeding your spirit truth, so that teachers add on to what you have.

CONCLUSION

If you decide to read the Bible for yourself, from cover-to-cover, there are just a few final remarks that I'd like to make on the Book, in general. Namely, the Holy Bible is NOT just a religion, and it's more than just a history book. It's a biography of Jesus Christ; it's God's UNCHANGING Words. It's a psychology book; and God's perfect plan for man is revealed. In life and death, the Bible teaches, comforts, encourages, civilizes, and disciplines those who may never read more than the Bible.

CHAPTER 2

7 REASONS WHY YOU SHOULD READ THE BIBLE FOR YOURSELF

FALSE RELIGIONS

The Bible on four different occasions, gives an account of the birth, death, and resurrection of Jesus Christ, as an ultimate sacrifice for man's sins. Since the Bible is the inspired Words of God, it is the Book of Truth. ANY doctrine that contradicts, speaks against, or denies the Word of God, found in the Holy Bible, IS A FALSE RELIGION.

This includes Judaism, which developed in biblical times. The basic teachings of this religion is that there is ONE God, who created the heavens and the earth, and delivered the Israelites out of bondage in Egypt. They believe that God alone should be worshipped. He's from everlasting to everlasting. He communicates to man through prophecy. Moses was the greatest prophet, and the Torah was revealed to Moses by God. And all of this is true. But these believers are still waiting for the Messiah to come! And that is their missing link.

God gave Moses His Laws. Throughout the Old Testament, man sinned consistently, and made SO MANY SACRIFICES to atone for their sins, that "sacrifice" and "atonement" lost their meaning in the eyes of God. It was like someone stepping on your toe every 15 minutes, and saying, "oops! I'm sorry." After hearing this so many times, the words undoubtedly lose their meaning---not to mention the numbness of your toes.

If you decide to read the Bible, you will see that such was the case in the Old Testament. God realized this system failed. As prophesied in the first Book of the Bible, God's new plan would send forth the Messiah to sacrifice His Life for the sins of man. Man needed only to confess that he was a sinner; be sorry in his heart; and believe that Jesus Christ died so that he could be free from sin. Accepting Jesus Christ as your personal Savior gives you new birth as God's Word promises many times.

Thus, if you encounter any man denying the deity of Christ, consult the Book that they used to develop and build their foundation on. But more importantly, remember that if a book has any discrepancies, there is truely no validity to the entire book. Yet, all of the many religions and cults that exist today, took something from the Bible to develop their own truth.

I was not able to get an accurate count on all the religions that exist today, but the number was definitely beyond this brief listing below. Still for further awareness on the various groups that exist, see the references in the Appendix.

RELIGIONS TODAY

New Thought
Unity
Devine Science
Roman Catholic
Protestant
Greek Orthodox
Universalists
Independent Baptist
Zoroastrianism
Islam
The Way
Eckankar
The Bhai'i Faith

Church of God
Pentecostal
Neo-Fundamentalists
Lutherans
Episcopalians
Presbyterians
Methodist
Nazarenes
Confucianism
Shinto
Iskcon
Jehovah Witness
Bha'gwan Shiree Rajneesh

Mormons
Friends
Humanists
Buddhists
Spiritualists
Hinduism
Jainism
Sikhism
Taoism
Est

THE SPREAD OF ISLAM

As the Islamic Movement is predicted to be the dominant religion in the world by the year 2000, it seems necessary and appropriate that I distinguish between their history and teachings and that of the Holy Bible, which I am encouraging you to read. This is especially important since the muslims have their own Book, called the Qur'an.

I've already mentioned the amazing formation of the Bible consisting of 50 different authors, inspired by God, living in (10) different countries; and the Bible being written over a 1,600-year span, with 52 Books compiled into one book, with a single, consistent theme!

On the other hand, Muhammad's background was of commercial experience, and not as humble as Jesus Christ's. Islam came into existence in a city, not in the wilderness. Mecca was a prosperous city, and the richer the people grew, the more socially dissatisfied they became. Emphasis was on personal possessions, and the here and now. Whereas, God's Word teaches you that worldly possessions are temporary, and the afterlife is what is everlasting---be it heaven or hell.

As time progressed, Muhammad copied the idea of judgment in the afterlife, and the concept grew into the Book of Works. Still, Muhammad's teachings reduced everything to a social issue, versus a spiritual level. The result was a teaching that wealth should be shared with the poor. While this is a morally wonderful concept, and the Muslims have made some phenominal accomplishments in the inner cities of the United States, the Bible clearly teaches that your works ALONE will NOT get you into heaven.

Other distinctions between the Holy Bible and the Qur'an are that the Qur'an is NOT historically based, and the few historical references made of Moses, Jesus, Noah all came from God's Word, and were already in existence. Muhammad knew nothing about prophecy in the

11

sense of the Old Testament. Instead, Islam is a religion of reform based on the teachings of Muhammad. The Qur'an also has no chronological order, in the sense of events occuring. As a result, the Qur'an speaks about visions, but there is NO verification as to whether they existed in the beginning of Muhammad's career or near the end.

If you wish to learn more about the Islamic Movement, I suggest you refer to the bibliography in the appendix. The final remarks I am going to make on this subject is that, the Qur'an makes references to the Holy Bible, but the Bible NEVER mentions the Qur'an. Whereas the Qur'an is a group of teachings, the Bible is NOT just a book of religion. It is God's revelation of himself to man in a course of history.

Muhammad founded the Islamic religion 1,350 years ago. "Muslim" means submission to the will of God or Allah. The essentials of Islam are known as the five pillars of Islam. (1) Muslims must declare that there is no God but Allah, and Muhammad is His Prophet. (2) Muslims must pray facing Mecca five times a day. (3) They must fast or not eat from sunrise to sunset during the Ramadan. (4) They must give to charity, and (5) go on a pilgrimage to Mecca. Sabbath is on Friday.

Although the muslims in general, are a very disciplined group, and they read their Qur'an more diligently than the average Christian reads their Bible, the sad fact remains---the Muslims DO NOT BELIEVE in the deity of Jesus Christ. Thus, they are a false religion. What does this mean? As they continue to grow, they are gathering multitudes of followers, and they are all heading straight to hell, if they don't stumble over the Truth before it's too late.

ISLAMIC TIME LINE
The chronology of the Islamic Movement is as follows:
570 - Birth of Muhammad
613 - Beginning of mission
622 - Muhammad emigrated to Medina
630 - Conquest of Mecca
632 - Death of Muhammad
635 - Conquest of Damascus
636 - Muslim Arab armies invaded the Holy Land
638 - Conquest of Jerusalem
639-42 Conquest of Egypt, Persia, beginning of conquest of North Africa
711-14 Conquest of Spain
732 - Battle of Poitiers
850 - Spread of Islam to Indonesia and China
970 - Construction of Al Azhar mosque, in Cairo
Post World War II - African American Muslims in the U.S. spread

WHY ISLAM IS SPREADING

There are primarily (7) reasons why Islam is spreading in the United States. First, Islam is growing because of the hypocrisy in the African American churches. The people at these churches are too involved with subtle bribery. For example, they go to church for their own selfish reasons. They want God to do something for them; maybe a new car, a job, a promotion. And the problem is there's too much "lip service," honoring God, and their hearts are far away. Other people get discouraged with the hypocrisy they see, and they go after a religion that seems to be more consistent and disciplined.

The second reason why Islam is spreading throughout America is because of the hypocrisy in the White churches. You can't say that you love Jesus, but hate African Americans or vice versa. God is love. You either have God and love all of His creations or you don't have enough God, so you can't love all of His creations. God loves all of us! He just hates our sins. So, when African American men learn that in order to become a member of the Ku Klux Klan, you must be a "born-again" Christian---this is a shock wave that will "send" any man running from "Christianity." Yet this outrageous hypocrisy and the many other contradictions that exist in white churches are distortions of the truth!

If you decide to read the Holy Bible, you will discover that God is NOT RACIST. He's loving, kind, forgiving, full of mercy, and a righteous Spirit! So, just as you should run from those teaching anything that promotes White Supremacy, you should also run from anyone who blatantly denounces the Word of God, calling it untruth and fairytales. My final comments on this note is don't be discouraged by the hypocrisy in the black churches or the white churches. Seek the Truth, because the Truth will set you free!

Another reason why Islam is growing rapidly is because of the absence of a father in the home. This is the most dangerous trend in America. Our children belong to God, and we must teach them the need for Jesus. Fathers must be present in the homes so that boys are properly disciplined, and grow up to fear and respect God as our Supreme Being. Fathers also serve as a role model offering guidance. For example, through good living example, fathers suggest, "Look son, we can survive and conquer, as long as we have God on our side." Also, "Look daughter, this is how you ought to be loved and treated, and the man you marry should love and reverence God."

When fathers are absent, our boys grow up as men prone to fear, insecurities, and depression. They grow up feeling defeated and wondering, "If my earthly father couldn't make it, how in the world can I?" Then, these sad, lost boys-to-men cling to ANYTHING that even offers a tiny ounce of hope. They need a protective figure, so they "huddle with their homies," get "high" and dance the hurt away. And if

13

the Islamic brothers hand them this "ray of hope" and even if they forget to stress the Ultimate Ray of Hope---God, the Father and His Son, Jesus Christ, many young men flock to the Islamic Movement.

But I tell you, the more brotherly love you need; the more sex and booze you need; and the more defeated you feel---the MORE YOU NEED JESUS! If you just accept Him, you'll witness the tumbling down of "prison walls." Thus, Islam sees all these weaknesses and hypocrisies and they capitalize on them. But you should read God's Word so that you will know the Truth.

Another reason why Islam is spreading is because Christians fail to missionize and evangelize to others. The Truth should be shared with everyone. Anyone who is suffering, struggling, or simply trying to handle life in their own strength needs to hear the Truth!

A fifth reason for Islam's growth is that Christians fail to realize their calling. Christians should ask God to use them and unveil their purpose. Why? Because each of us are spiritually gifted with something special: singing, teaching, leadership, writing, speaking, etc. We are suppose to use our spiritual gifts to point others to Christ, and glorify God. This is our only purpose on earth. It is through this servitude that we receive our earthly blessings. Yet, we miss our blessings and we fall short of God's glory when we do otherwise, and the result is an increasing population of false religions.

The final two reasons why Islam is growing and will continue to grow is that we've developed an egocentric character. Instead of us seeking to serve God, we're waiting for God to serve us! We want to be all important, so WE FORGET that we are NOTHING WITHOUT GOD, but EVERYTHING WITH HIM. Also, we compromise our personal testimony. We don't even count our blessings, so we certainly are not in the mind-frame to tell others about the goodness of Christ and what He has done for us lately.

As a result of the hypocrisy, absenteeism of fathers, failure to missionize, serve God diligently, and give our personal testimonies---the world we live in is sinking deeply into sin. We're being swamped by false religions and cults. We live in total chaos, and from time-to-time we actually EXPECT news of incidences like the one in Waco, Texas.

WHAT'S A SOLUTION?

I have several suggestions on how Christians can make a difference. But then I will conclude and return to my title and purpose and theme of this book **Why Every Man Should Read The Bible From Cover-to-Cover, At Least Once** . I first want to comment that because Christians have already won the victory over this life, through the blood of Jesus Christ, it's all the more reason why they should be out evangelizing in greater multitudes. If they are not, it is either because they are not being properly and thoroughly taught; they are not serious enough about their commitment to God; or sad to say, they are not really Christians. It is not for me to say who is or isn't a true Christian. But I can say, as a Christian, in love, that there is a definite wrong in the picture of a man or woman, who's called themself a Christian for 25-30 years. Yet, the only souls they managed to save or the seeds they planted were that of their offspring, which were literally forced to come from Jesus. This is sad, because in this amount of time, your ACTIONS ALONE should have attracted AT LEAST (3) people per year to the Light of Jesus! That means in 30-years of serving the Lord, 90 more people KNOW THE LORD because of something you said or did, or something you didn't say or do! In any event, your 30-years weren't wasted. But back to the subject---there are three definite responsibilities that Christians can take on to add to the solution of the world's problems.

The three responsibilities of Christians that will make a difference are that they make a personal COMMITMENT to GOD; cease the hypocrisy; and read God's Word in its entirety. By definition, commitment means to make a pledge, or to compromise oneself. In order to compromise oneself to God, there must be a heart's desire for righteousness and truth. Without this personal desire, a commitment will be difficult, if not next to impossible. It is the level of commitment that brings forth results. For example, your commitment to God enables you to pray over even the most minute decisions, which helps you make better life choices. This includes working at a marriage versus resorting to a divorce; forgiving a loved one versus holding a grudge; and even giving up a high-paying job position, to work for the Lord. If you make a true commitment to God to live for His glory, you will be a living example, and your lifestyle alone will be a testimony for God.

When you're walking in the spirit of God, you have a more loving, joyful, peaceful, and kind spirit. Who wouldn't be attracted to such a light? Furthermore, greater multitudes of Christians walking in the Spirit of God would mean more kindness, peace, joy, and love in the world; And who can argue that this world is NOT in need of more love and peace?

Unlike Muslims, many believers in Jesus Christ don't make Christianity their way of life, by committing to God, and the result is hypocrisy. There's a lot to be said about hypocrisy---what it is, common examples, why it's so very wrong, and why it's necessary that we cease being hypocrites. I summed it all up in the following poem:

HYPOCRISY

Hypocrites -
They're the ones who sin til a pool of blood
trails behind them from all those they killed
Then they repent, rise above the world

So that THEY can look down on the world and Judge them.

Yes, the hypocrite is the one
who embraces and calls many Christian women, "daughter"
But the one she really birthed
She can't even sit down with and comfortably chat over tea.
What is this about, "I love you, but I got to go."
Yet God sits patiently and listens to all of us.
And you say, "I want to be godly."
If you are sincere, you'll say
"God is that me? If it is, please help me."
And isn't that a hypocrite who sends her son to hell
because he's sinned one time too many.
She's judged him as doomed
when God is so much more full of mercy.
God is patiently waiting for His son to cry out to Him for help
Just so that He can show some compassion.

But the real Christian's function is to go to the lost,
in love, and share the love of Jesus with the lost.
This is our only purpose.
If believers stay huddled together
and never mingle among the lost to continuously point towards the Light,
We defeat our purpose for being here.
We just as well go on to a Higher Place.
Our lives are complete!
Beware! Because hypocrites not only fail to serve God
by sharing the Gospel that "Jesus loves you,"
and sharing this with those that Don't Know,
But in selfishly rejoicing in the Lord
and condeming those who don't follow the Lord--
Our Judgment makes these lost souls defensive.
They run from us!
The lost souls feel like,
"If loving God is about self-righteousness
and showing no compassion..."
Then you hypocrites are guilty of a horrible crime.
The crime is that you turned someone against God and His Word.
The lost soul ran from his conviction
without learning about the love of Jesus and His mercy.
Hypocrites promote the destruction of our nation
because the lost is crying out (through rage and fear)
and saying, "You Christians don't understand."
Instead of the "Christians" listening and trying to understand,

and praying,
The "Christians" say, "GO TO HELL!"
They shout this even BEFORE they hear what God wants them to say
or do.

I say to you "Hypocrites"
If you really love Jesus and want to be like Him,
Then STOP judging as if you were God.
Ask God to teach you COMPASSION FOR THE LOST
Ask God to help you to STOP TURNING YOUR BACK ON THE LOST-
. . . those who need Jesus.
Ask God to teach you what to say or not say
And what to do or not do.
Ask this of your Heavenly Father
or else, look in the mirror with brown tarnished teeth
And grin as you say, "Oh, I'm just the hypocrite.
I can keep my dirt with me.
I don't have to come clean."
Dearest friends,
I write to you this poem in prayer
that you will periodically make a conscious effort
to reflect on your words, thoughts, and actions as a Christian.

My suggestion to you that can make a difference is that you read
God's Word from cover-to-cover, at least once. Going to Sunday
Church Services, weekday Bible Study, staying in prayer, and uplifting
your fellow-Christians through words and deeds, are outward signs of
your commitment to God. But your spiritual growth comes from a
deeper level of interacting with God. As I said before, commitment
results from a heart's desire for truth and righteousness. If your heart
really desires truth, there's only ONE SOURCE--the Word of God.

When you commit to 30-minutes or one hour of reading, or 1-3
chapters of reading daily, it is at this moment that you have really
made a commitment to God. Afterall, how can you pray diligently or
praise and worship an unfamiliar Spirit? How can you serve a
Stranger, except that you first come to know Him and what He
expects?

I know I said this already, but this is the FIRST TIME I'm laying
MY opinions out before the public---MY CLIENTS. And I'm really
delighting in this occasion! My final conclusion on this note is that you
either want God and His Word, or you don't! If you've decided, it's a
perfect time to read the Bible from cover-to-cover. And if you read
about 3 chapters per day or 23 chapters per week, you can comfortably read the Bible in one year. If you're still undecided about giving
your life to Christ after one year, at least you'll have the truth in you,

which will enable you to choose a Bible-Teaching church if the need arise. You'll aslo recognize false doctrine if it comes before you. You'll know how to live in peace and joy, if you desire it. And you'll know what God expects of you, if you care to accept it. In essence, you have NOTHING to lose and EVERYTHING to gain.

7 REASONS WHY YOU SHOULD READ FOR YOURSELF

This book is in no way intended to discredit or take anything away from the teachings of preachers and Bible study teachers. If it did, then it would have to devalue the entire New Testament, including Paul's instructions to Titus and the many churches he set up in Rome, Corinth, and Ephesus, to name a few. In addition, this book would be a total contradiction to the Word of God, since He, himself, ordained teachers to guide us through His Scriptures.

Still, taking nothing away from church sermons and Bible study classes, every man should read the Bible for himself. There are (7) Seven primary reasons why.

The first and foremost reason you should read the Bible in its entirety is because **GOD'S WORDS SAY YOU SHOULD**. For example, 2Timothy 2:15 says that you should, "Study to show thyself approved unto God, a workman that needeth not to be ashamed, rightly dividing the word of truth." If you are ignorant of God's Word, you stand dumb before Satan's friends, and your dumbfoundedness is what makes you shameful. For example, how many ADULTS have literally hid behind their windows and doors at the sighting of a Jehovah Witness? Yet, if you knew God's Word, you could politely and confidently invite the Witness in, "present" them with the truth, and witness them fleeing from you or to Christ! In summary, you need God's Word to stand before His enemies.

Acts 17:11 tells you about a church that read the Scriptures for themself, when Paul said, "These were more noble than those in Thessalonica, in that they received the word with all readiness of mind, and searched the Scriptures daily, whether those things were so." They verified their teachings. Psalm 119 gives you further encouragement to read God's Word and pray for understanding. This Psalmist was inspired by the beauty of God's law and he was led to write this love poem. But Acts 8:26-40 best summarizes my argument. The verses are about the conversion of an Ethiopian. He's depicted reading God's Word and being questioned about his understanding of it. The Ethiopian believes he can only gain understanding through the guidance of a teacher. However, the very Scriptures that he was reading challenged that thought, because they described someone being led as a sheep to slaughter, and because of their ignorance was defenseless.

If you read these verses, you will learn that EVERY born-again Christian is sent a Holy Spirit to be their God-given teacher. As this is true, it has been my personal experience that when you read the Bible for yourself, you are double blessed because a teacher simply adds on to what you've already fed your Spirit! In light of this, Acts 8:26-40 describes your weakened position if you don't read the Bible for yourself, and tells you why you CAN read it.

The second reason why you should read the Bible for yourself is because **GOD REVEALS HIMSELF TO MAN THROUGH HIS WORD**. And I could write a book on WHY you should WANT this revelation, but I'll contain my list to a few reasons. God created the universe; He's a healer; He's the reason why you breathe each new day; He loves you even as you sin; and His mercies endure forever! These are reasons enough why you should want to get to know Him. But for those of you who recognize God's awesome powers, how can you truly serve God or even live a godly life, UNLESS YOU KNOW HIM? Ephesians 5:1-2 tells you to "Follow God's example in everything we do, just as a child imitates his or her father." But you cannot follow His example unless you know His ways. This comes from reading God's Word.

For almost 30 years I knew OF God, based on what people led me to believe . But I was amazed at how different God is from what I was told, and truly, the word "awesome" is an understatement! The entire Old Testament paints a really explicit picture of WHO GOD IS. I believe it is this picture that makes you want to have a more intimate relationship with Him.

Another reason why God's revelation of himself to man is important is because you learn what God expects of you. For example, in His Word, He makes very definite distinctions between true Christian conduct, legalism, and hypocrisy. The most valuable lesson you can learn from getting to know God is that His ways really simplifies life, and it is our sins which complicate it.

A third reason why you should read the Bible in its entirety is because **GOD'S WORD INCREASES FAITH**. According to Hebrews 11:1, "Faith is the substance of things hoped for, the evidence of things not seen." In other words, it is the confident assurance that something you want is waiting for you, even though there are NO VISIBLE SIGNS. Examples of faith include God speaking the world into existence with words and faith. Enoch trusted God so much that God took him to heaven without his having to die first. A final example of faith is that there were no signs of a flood, and yet Noah believed God's warning and built an ark that saved his family's life.

Since God doesn't guarantee you a life of luxury and ease, faith is by no means easy. I can attest to this because it was faith that enabled me to author this book! My circumstances of eviction notices, disconnected telephone, broken car, no car, marital discord, and no job---were BEYOND BLEAK! Yet, God told me to write this book, and

19

faith alone carried me through. And God's work was done. Still, there is a greater benefit of having faith. Faith builds strong character, and it is THIS STRENGTH that enables you to have inner peace and joy in the midst of the worst storm. Truly, faith is a gift from God.

So then, how does God's Word increase your faith? For a moment, let's take away God's Word and use something as basic as music. If you were forced to hear the same song 2-3 times per day, everyday for one month, you would know the song. And whether you liked the song or not, it would be so much a part of you that you would likely find yourself humming the tune. The music radio industry confirms this opinion, because they play "hit" songs throughout the day, and you inevitably find yourself singing songs that you may not even like.

With regards to God, if you know little or nothing of His existence, and you began to read the Bible each day, you will see and hear so much of Him in the Book, that His very existence comes alive and becomes a part of you. Moreover, if you commit to reading the Bible in one year, the experience will captivate you; engross you in history; Proverbs will stimulate your mind. Psalms will encourage and comfort you; and you will witness God's ever-presence (historically, presently, and in the future). Thus, one year of reading God's Word in its entirety fills your spirit with God Himself. As John 1:1 teaches you that God is the Word and the Word is God, the more Word you put inside of you, the more God you're taking in, and the more your faith increases.

So far, I've concluded that you should read the Bible because (1) the Bible tells you to; (2) God reveals himself to man through His Word, and you should want to know God because He is the VERY REASON why YOU BREATHE; and (3) God's Word increases faith, which builds your character.

The fourth reason why you should read the Bible is because it is the Book of Truth, and when you have this PROTECTIVE SWORD, **NO FALSE TEACHER CAN MISLEAD YOU.** This is extremely critical in a society that's growing increasingly liberal and cults are on the uprise.

I can attest to God's Word being a "protective sword," because I once entered a Christian Science library out of curiosity. The staff person was extremely pleasant, and I'm just a glutton for kind people! The librbary room was bright, neat, and filled with Holy Bibles and books by a female figure who was the all-knowing authority on interpreting and teaching the Bible. This was the first time I entered a "free, public library" filled with books by two primary authors! Without elaborating on the teachings of the Christian Science religion, I just thank God and give Him all the praises and glory that I had ENOUGH TRUTH in me NOT to be led astray.

Truly, false teachings can be a life-death situation. And when I say this, I'm forced to reflect back on my early childhood friend. She and I were raised in the same non-teaching baptist church. The difference is, I sought the truth for myself as an adult, and today, she is in Alabama in a religious cult that has claimed the life of one of her babies! This story does more than just give me chills down my spine. Tears run down my face and my heart grieves. But what else can I say, other than God does not command us to kill our babies; and that God's GOODNESS is revealed in His Word.

God's laws teach you EVERYTHING you need to know to get through life, and God made the laws for man's sake! The problem is when you get engrossed in man's laws, you find yourself in ritual praying, ritual fasting, and ritual almsgiving. Such rituals give you inner strength, a sense of pride, self-gratification, and there's just too much emphasis on self. This rigidity does NOT allow your personal relationship with God to transpire. There's absolutely NOTHING WRONG with praying five times a day, EXCEPT that you should be led into prayer by the Holy Spirit---NOT BY THE REQUIREMENTS OF A MAN-MADE RELIGION.

If you truly believe in God and want spiritual growth, why not seek Him through His Word, since this is the source of Truth. God's Word should show you that ANY religion that emphasizes self-autonomy, self-sufficiency, and SELF, in general, is against God and also false. The reason is God is the only one who is almighty. He is all-knowing, able to sustain you, prosper you and heal you. He alone is worthy to be praised.

In essence, all that I'm saying is READ GOD'S WORD so that you are not mislead by man's false teaching. Also, it doesn't seem practical to participate in any religion that takes something from the Bible to formulate a new "truth," when you can go directly to the Book and get EVERYTHING you need to know.

Another reason to read the Bible for yourself is **MAN IS PRONE TO ERROR, SO YOU CAN'T RELY SOLELY ON HIM.** Unlike the fourth reason, which emphasized false teachers who blatantly denied God's Word and created their own truths, this fifth reason places emphasis on the possibility of innocent human error. This becomes a problem when you collectively gather an abundance of human errors and they become the basis of your truths. The root of the problem lies in your inability to fend off these errors because you lack wisdom that comes from the Scriptures.

Here's an example to illustrate my point. A teacher's job is to add on to your foundation (which is common sense and your brain). As such, when you were just a child in elementary school, your teacher didn't give you a brain. She simply gave you knowledge to feed your brain. As a result, if any teacher told you something outrageous like, "Jump out of a window because you can fly," you had enough sense to challenge her. This is an extreme example, but the point is you NEED a foundation BEFORE you can RELY on a teacher.

Similarly, man does not give you a Holy Spirit. This comes from God through acceptance of His Son. Once you have the Holy Spirit in you, YOU should feed it truth that comes from the Word of God. Then, when you go before teachers, they simply add on depth and under-standing to your foundation.

Am I saying that you will know and memorize EVERY Scripture and lesson of the Bible in a single experience? Absolutely not. What I am saying is that when you read the Bible in its entirety, you get truth inside of you which reappears as it is needed, if it's needed.

In summary, the purpose of the fourth reason is to protect you from the enemy---Satan. And the purpose of the fifth reason is to RELY MORE ON THE HOLY SPIRIT to give you truth, than on your-self or another man. That brings us to the last two reasons why every man should read the Bible from cover-to-cover for himself. The sixth reason is **YOU GAIN SELF AWARENESS**, and the seventh reason is **YOU LEARN THE TRUE MEANING OF LOVE**, which is God's great-est commandment (Matthew 22:37).

You may wonder, "If God reveals Himself to man through His Word, why does man need SELF-AWARENESS?" By reading the Bible, beginning with Adam and Eve, and ending in Revelations, you see the true, consistently evil nature of man. He's depicted as disobe-dient, self-righteous, greedy, prideful, jealous, selfish, violent, lustful, and everything that's opposite of God. And the purpose of reflecting on this is NOT to condemn man, but to show him how very much he NEEDS CHRIST. Also, in taking an in-depth look at human nature, this helps you to choose whether or not you want to live a life of good or evil, based on more information and understanding. Finally, through self-awareness, you learn to have more compassion for others, because you recognize that EVERYBODY'S PROBLEM IS THE SAME---THEY NEED MORE GOD!

Finally, you should read the Bible for yourself, because it illus-trates the **TRUE MEANING OF LOVE**. Since lack of love causes the breakdown of family structures, wars, senseless killings, and basically the destruction of the earth, it seems VERY NECESSARY that you learn what true love consists of. Then you can fulfill God's greatest commandment. Think of it. If there was more love in your life, you wouldn't have a sexual identity crisis that leads to homosexuality and bisexuality. You wouldn't be sexually promiscuous, posing the threat of diseases and death. You wouldn't have endless abortions; and you wouldn't have angry young men killing innocent babies and children as if they were flies---with no remorse.

The ultimate demonstration of love is shown throughout the Bible. For example, when GOD DELIVERS the Israelites out of Egypt; when

GOD CONTINUOUSLY RESCUES MAN EVERYTIME he disobeys and falls; when GOD HEALS the sick , and FEEDS THE HUNGRY--- these are just SOME examples of God's kind acts of love. But even as you reflect on your life today, you give little or none of your time to God. Yet, He blesses you with life, which is an opportunity to be better today than yesterday. Through the examples in the Bible, you learn that true love is unconditional, and beyond reasoning. It is also a choice. Though man is disobedient, rebellious, and undeserving, God chooses to love him anyway. As such, read the Bible and let God be your example of how to love. Then choose to love God and His creations!

CHAPTER 3

WHAT DID THE BIBLE DO FOR ME?

MY LOVE TESTIMONY

I know that I've said this several times already, but I have to say it again! This is the first time that I'm opening up, publicly offering MY OPINIONS and at the same time, expressing ME. All my life I've been relatively quiet and shy, smiling at the public I adored, and uttering words about business, when the occasion would arise. But today, I'm giving you my testimonies!

It gives me sheer joy to share with you what the Lord has done for me through His Word. In addition, this book has been my outlet to release the excitement that's inside of me. But what's in it for you? Hopefully you will gain really wonderful lessons from my testimonies, so that if you choose to never in life open a Bible, you'll be at liberty of using the wisdom I gained. But the ultimate objective of my testimonies is to inspire you to want to experience the Book for yourself. . . and you too, will fall in love with God, our Heavenly Father, and His Son, Jesus Christ.

As chapter two ended on a love note, I'd like to elaborate on the subject of love, through my first testimony. But to talk about love, I have to reflect on my childhood for background purposes. First of all, I was the only girl of two brothers, and the youngest of three. I was raised and very much loved. I was dressed like a living doll; I got taken on lots of trips; ate at fine restaurants on a weekly basis; was encouraged and praised beyond measure; and literally put on a pedestal by my mother, babysitter, and two brothers. The fact of the matter is, I was "loved" too much!

I got very minimum discipline. But I can remember very vividly witnessing my younger brother taking several beatings that should have been for me. I can remember my two brothers going on punishment for a glass door that I kicked in because of my bad temper. And I can remember getting no disciplinarian actions taken against me for throwing lye on my brother in a fit of rage! The trips I took to South of the Border, Disney World, and Disney Land didn't include my brothers. And I don't remember them getting the praises that I consistently heard.

Without digging deeper into my PERFECT CHILDHOOD, the point I want to make is that, as a child, I subconsciously suppressed deep hurt, sadness, and guilt over my special treatment. I carried this guilt into my adult life, and as a result, I have a very "undeserving spirit" that I'm gradually being delivered from.

What I mean by "undeserving spirit" is that I ABSOLUTELY LOVE giving to others---be it research assistance, typing, cooking, babysitting, and you name it! If you need help and I can help you, it gives me absolute pleasure to oblige. And you are probably saying, "That doesn't sound like a problem." But the problem lies in my inability to receive as freely as I give. On the surface, the problem seems like a pride issue, but it's really quite the opposite.

As a result of this problem, I've been in really tight financial binds, and although there were people that I could go to, I just wouldn't. For example, my father once offered me a sum of money that he'd been saving for me. I declined the offer, and told him that I was just happy to be with him, and that was the truth. But at the time he offered me money, I was facing a court date for eviction. Even though the eviction would have put me and my two children out on the streets, I just couldn't dream of asking my darling father for help. I think I would rather have died first. This was an absolute extreme case of how my spirit wouldn't allow me to ask for help.

Once upon a time, God planted a deep, unshakeable love in my heart for someone, and because I didn't think I was worthy of his love, I ran from my blessing. Then, there have been times when I've borrowed $5 to $20 from my mother or friends, and it literally pained me to my heart to have to go to them for a loan. In any event, this undeserving spirit was unnatural, unhealthy, and certainly NOT from God.

It was during my reading of the Bible that I was able to even recognize that I had this problem. But more than that, I recognized a solution---God's love! I noticed that as bad as we may behave, and as undeserving as we may be, God loves us dearly. And He blesses us because He loves us. So it's okay to receive as well as give.

Today, I have a deeper awareness of God's love, and a love letter that I got from God, through the Holy Spirit, made me realize for the FIRST TIME IN MY LIFE, that I'M LOVABLE. It was my acceptance of God's love that gave me the courage to open up and express myself freely! It was also God's love that gave me the desire to want to please Him, because of HOW He loved me. I wanted to be cleansed and obedient to God's Word.

As I read the Bible, I grew spiritually, but my fleshly desires didn't just stop or go away. The difference is, without God in the center of my life, I gave in to temptations. Now, when I am tempted, I confess it to God. I go straight to my Heavenly Father and I spill my guts by confessing everything in my heart. This relieves me, soothes me, and God keeps me from giving in to temptations. Each time God comforts me and keeps me safe, it is a reminder of the love He has for me and all of His children, despite who we are---sinners.

God's love inspired many poems in me. But this one in particular just came to mind:

GOD'S LOVE

We were so undeserving
Yet, God loved us
so deeply and completely.

When we conceive
SOME of God's Love
we want to just
embrace someone
and say, "Jesus loves you!"

Deep gratitude,
peace and joy
pops out of our skin,
and we want to share it
with others. . .

A Christian mate
is a perfect way
to express God's Love!

The only other comment I want to make on this subject is that the Bible sold me on the love of Jesus Christ!

WHAT GOD EXPECTS OF YOU AND ME

God loves us and He has a perfect plan for each of our lives. Although He allows us to make choices, He really does want us to build an intimate, Father-child relationship, by believing on His Word, obeying His laws, and staying in communion with Him through prayer. And what God expects from us more than anything is obedience.

Obedience is important because there are many people who study the Bible for 20 to 30 years or even more. Yet, they compromise with the Scriptures for momentary pleasures, such as adultery, lust, or they hold onto ungodly traits such as insecurities and jealousy.

Jealousy acted out in a marriage relationship is very hurtful to the accused, because it's like an assault on their character and integrity. The Bible clearly speaks against envy and jealousy. And anything the Bible speaks against, that you knowingly and willingly do, and even go so far as to justify your actions, is an offense to God. You have a CHOICE to offend God and hurt your mate, or you can choose to take your insecurities to God in prayer. This is your God-given choice. But disobeying God's Word hinders your spiritual growth, which keeps you from experiencing total peace and joy. In addition, this and other ungodly conduct discourages others from growing in the Lord. Thus, God allows you to choose to be good or evil, but He really EXPECTS obedience. Knowing His Word isn't enough. You must live it!

MY PERSONAL GROWTH TESTIMONY

As I recognized SOME of the depths of God's love, His awesomeness mesmerized me! My love for my Heavenly Father deepened in such a way that I sought Him daily for instructions. Although my prayer life was already active, it increased. I began to pray over the simplest things, but I learned that if you pray about everything, you can NEVER go wrong. For example, I was one day planning to buy an outfit for my mother's 25th job anniversary. As I browsed through a store, I said, "God, what color should I buy?" God, through the Holy Spirit said, "Wait. Don't buy anything." I continued to browse. I was tempted to buy a purple suit, but I followed my spirit. As a result, my mother called me on the telephone that evening and said, "My anniversary colors are black and white. If you can, wear those colors." I, of course, gave God all the glory for answering my prayers promptly in the store. Not only did God save me from buying the wrong color, but He also saved me money, because I already had a nice black jumper, and a white blouse to wear under it! From that small lesson, I learned that it pays to pray! And it pays to obey.

As I read the Bible and observed man's behavior, I began to do some serious self-examination, and the discoveries were some serious ills. Just as I prayed for daily instructions, I began to pray and ask God to unveil my areas of weaknesses and cleanse me. God answered this prayer, too. But the picture He presented me with wasn't pretty at all.

God showed me, at different occasions during my reading of the Bible, that I was very tempermental in the worst way. I was selfish. I needed to learn the importance of forgiving. I needed desperately to learn patience. I was worshipping false gods, and I needed to learn self-control. Some of these lessons were very painful. But because of the gentleness and beauty of God, He blessed me with wisdom and understanding as He cleansed me.

Bad temperment is the first cleansing experience I want to talk about. First of all, the Holy Spirit showed me that a bad temper was like an ugly monster filled with vicious rage. I felt like this very monster whenever all of my deeply suppressed ANGER flaired. I felt more like this monster because I had repeatedly vivid dreams of shooting and killing people and awakening with a sense of relief, as if I had just delivered a baby. Although they were just dreams, murder should have placed in me a sense of fear, anxiety, and remorse. Instead, I felt refreshed! On top of recognizing the magnitude of anger that was inside of me, and the dreams I was having, I also desired a gun. Without leading you to believe that I was once crazy, the point I want to make is that the Holy Spirit showed me the ugliness of my temper. And I certainly wouldn't make it into Heaven with that kind of evilness in my heart!

WHERE DID MY ANGER COME FROM?
Where did my anger that turned into deep rage REALLY sprang

from? Was it ALL from being treated special, leading me to FEEL like I had stolen love from my darling brothers? Did some of it come from the absence of my father and not understanding why? Did the anger come from my stepfather offering me $15 for oral sex, when I was only 11 or 12 years old? And what was the worst part of the offer? Was it broken trust or was it FEELING like my mother either didn't believe me or she didn't care?

I don't know where my temper came from. I just know it was like a bad nightmare! There was so much junk squashed in my belly. The junk started out as deep hurt. Since I never dealt with the hurt, I just piled more "stuff" on top of it. I used my "strength," "intelligence," and my determination, which everybody called my "stubbornness," and I grinded the junk into a really TIGHT BALL! The problem is, if someone touched a sore spot, I exploded and I was capable of killing them, if given the opportunity.

What did the Bible do for me? God didn't just take away my temper and anger. He helped me to understand the root of my anger. He showed me that anger was okay for a moment, but not good to hold onto; that even He got angry. The greatest thing that God did was He taught me how to handle my anger, and bless others at the same time! Truly, God is more than awesome. Before taking away my anger, God showed me that not only was I holding on to anger, but I was continually adding on. For example, I chose to marry someone who SEEMED feminine in nature, and I didn't care because I felt deserving of a less-than-perfect mate. Then, as I grew spiritually, I wanted a God-loving, God-fearing mate, and I got angry. By the grace of God and His Word, I was able to understand why I was angry and the truth set me FREE! Today, the Bible helps me to make more responsible choices. I try to confront my hurts BEFORE they turn into anger; and when all else fails, I go to God in prayer.

WHERE DOES ALL THE ANGER COME FROM?

As I read the Bible and witnessed how Adam and Eve ruined a completely perfect plan that God had for man, I saw injustice. When I read about how the Israelites continuously disobeyed God, and blamed God for their sufferings, because of choices THEY MADE, I saw more injustice. When I witnessed how the Israelites called on God repeatedly, and He answered their calls by blessing them through the wilderness, and the Israelites didn't even acknowledge their blessings, let alone appreciate them, I saw more injustice. As I witnessed the sins of man throughout the Old Testament, and how God never changed, but loved and blessed man even as he sinned, I felt deeply saddened and recognized more injustice.

God, in His patience, recognized this old system of laws and rituals had failed. He introduced a new plan which sent His Son as an ultimate sacrifice for man's sins. In this new plan, man needed to believe on God's Son and accept Him as Lord and Savior. Many people even rejected this awesome plan, and this is an ultimate injustice.

Through these historical events, God, through His Word, taught me that at the root of ANY anger is deep hurt; and at the root of deep hurt is an INJUSTICE. This valuable lesson enabled me to reflect on everyone who made me angry and understand why. The understandings brought forth truths, and the truths set me FREE of my anger.

Although understanding anger can free us, sometimes getting the truth about why someone hurt you is not so easy. That's where my awesome blessing came in! God taught me to write out my ANGER everytime it flaired. Writing about injustices would relieve me; teach others how not to be; and in the interim, point them to Christ. So while God presented an ugly side of me, He blessed me with understanding, and further blessed me with wisdom on how to constructively handle my problems, using my spiritual gift!

Since EVERYBODY has different spiritual gifts, my suggestion to you is that you pray and ask God to reveal your spiritual gifts so that you, too can constructively handle your ungodly behavior, and bless others along the way. Perhaps you're an artist, a painter, a singer, a dancer, a teacher. . . only God knows!

I WAS SELFISH, TOO

The next monster that God revealed to me was my selfishness. This was the most painful lesson that I learned, and the one that I took the longest to heal from. First of all, because of my very "generous" nature, let me tell you, I was shocked to even learn that I was, in fact, selfish. Before I talk about why selfishness is so wrong, and how I demonstrated selfishness to others, let me make a distinction between generosity and selfish-giving.

Generosity is by definition, nobleness of the soul; liberal, or free-spirited. If you are generous in a noble sense, you give out of the kindness of your heart, AND with the intent of giving someone something that they desire or TRUELY NEED. Moreover, when you give in a noble sense, you have the recipients' best interest at heart. Selfish-giving, on the other hand, is for a stroking of the ego; or for self-gratification; or it can be done out of convenience. For example, some people give because it makes them feel important. Some people give because it soothes their guilty conscience. Others may give because they lack storage space, or simply have items that they don't want, and it's convenient to give them away. My point here is that once upon a time, I use to take my credit cards and my friends, and go on wild shopping sprees. Because I did this, I THOUGHT that I was generous. But, in truth, I did NOT have my friends' best interest at heart when I took them shopping. I took them shopping because I was feeling sad. I wanted to feel good; and I wanted to have some fun! They were conveniently available, the credit cards were at hand, and they went for the ride! My friends didn't suffer any loss from this selfish-giving experience. I just want to illustrate that at those precise moments, I was NOT being generous. I was giving my self gratification.

God used a dream that brought me back to my early childhood, to painfully show me that I was SELFISH. God showed me that momma Brown, my babysitter, was like a second mother to me. She was very strict about table manners. She stressed the importance of saying, "Good morning" and respecting people's household, by never tracking dirt into their homes. She taught me the importance of saving money. Each day, she cooked and fed me meals fit for a queen. This included a hot, full course breakfast EVERYDAY; and for dinner she baked homemade loaves of bread, fried chicken, made cabbage, beans and rice, macaroni and cheese, homemade dumplings, homemade pound cakes, bread pudding, and the list just goes on and on!

The main point here is that this "babysitter" cooked and fed me like this EVERYDAY! And if this wasn't enough, Momma Brown gave me a sense of respect for all cultures. She introduced me to her Cuban friends and gave me cuban foods. She took me to Pennsylvania Dutch Country once a year. She took me to Italian restaurants. Every Saturday, she took ME to the movies and out for a steak dinner in New York City. On top of all this royal treatment, she paid me to clean her furniture and taught me how to save money. Momma Brown praised me and gave me words of encouragement from ages 4 to 12. I did nothing to deserve this special treatment. She just treated me like a queen.

What was the worst part of this picture? As much of an impact as she has on me this very day, I grew up and NEVER went back to say, "I remember. . " "Thank you, " "You're always in my heart," "How are you feeling today?" NOTHING!!! In my adult life, I saw Momma Brown maybe twice. I didn't call her once a week, once a month, once a year, or even every five years! Six years ago, Momma Brown died, and all I could do was go to her funeral and weep, and say, "I'm so sorry." I NEVER FORGOT her. I always carried her in my heart. But SHE NEVER KNEW!

Momma Brown passed in 1990. It was 1995 when I had a dream of her visiting me. God forced me to look at our relationship, and I wept hysterically. God showed me all the people I had since treated similarly. The purpose was NOT to give me more guilt, but to awaken me to what I was---SELFISH. My selfishness had to do with me giving my SELF and my time. I was withdrawn, so I had dearly loved friends and family members that I would see every 3-8 years!

The valuable, but very painful lessons I learned was that (1)self-ishness brings deep shame and regrets. (2)You cannot completely serve God if you are selfish, because that is what enables you to sin, (thinking more of your self than God). (3)In order to overcome selfishness, you must forsake SELF, and this requires discipline and self-control. Have I graduated from this lesson? Not yet.

I know that I still have layers of selfishness on me because not many months ago, I reflected on some marital problems I was having, and my unhappiness inspired me to write a horrible poem about God. I say horrible because I compared my Heavenly Father to an intravenous needle! "Life sustaining and sufficent, but clear, flavorless, colorless, and unexciting." This was so horribly far from the truth! God is full of flavor and MORE than enough! Needless to say, I had some serious repenting to do.

The important lesson that I learned from this poem was that WE get so consumed with OUR problems and what WE want, that we lose sight of God's goodness. Truly, selfishness also blinds us of God's TRUE, UNCHANGING BEAUTY.

FORGIVENESS IS NECESSARY

As the Bible teaches about the importance of forgiving, I learned that I needed to learn how to forgive MYSELF, as well as others. As badly as you may behave, if you are SORRY in your heart, and you ask God to forgive you--He does. Therefore, if God, the Supreme Being, can forgive you, who are you NOT to forgive? The implications are that you are MORE than GOD, if He can forgive you and you don't have to.

If you don't forgive yourself, you may spend a lifetime feeling guilty about your past. Your guilt may cause you to inflict pain on yourself or just reject God's wonderful blessings. Inability to forgive others leads to grudges and grudges are a form of bondage. For example, holding a grudge is like being in a prison camp chained to a gate. Each time you encounter your offender, there's tension; a flair-up of old anger; bitterness; and a firm grip on something dead. Something is dead when it's of the past, and nothing in life can bring it back. The problem with holding on to something "dead" is that you're NOT FREE to enter anything new that life has to offer. For example, life offers lasting joy, peace, happiness, love, warmth, and comfort.

Bondage that keeps you holding a grudge can very easily be broken with forgiveness. It's as simple as looking the offender in the eye and saying, "That deeply hurt me." Then recognize that you can't undo the hurt, and allow it to be healed by NEVER again clinching for it. As long as you keep your hands off of the hurt, after you acknowledge it, and accept that you can't relive the moment, you can heal and forgive. Forgiveness sets you free!

Forgiveness also builds character. For example, when you forgive others, you are less likely to be consumed with THEIR weaknesses. This also lessens your chances of feeling sadness, depression, and anger.

Imagine yourself as a committed, loyal partner, and your spouse just up and leaves you for no apparent reason. You will likely feel resentment, anger, disappointment, rejection, etc. As time goes on, you may heal some and suppress the remains of your feelings. You will likely get enough courage to enter a new relationship down the road.

The problem is, if you NEVER totally forgive your ex-husband or wife for their injustice, you will likely bring insecurities into your new relationship. Your bondage will likely cause you to act out in jealousy, which as I mentioned before, hurts the innocent victim. Unfortunately, your inability to let go of the past blinds you from seeing your partner in truth. Your feelings of rejection, inadequacy, and insecurity hinders your new relationship. You can't give ALL of yourself and love your new mate freely and totally. Again, I say forgiveness breaks this bondage. As a result, you learn obedience to God's Word, and you also reap the benefits of obedience, which are peace, joy, and love.

Although I am not a grudgeful person, I have certainly inflicted myself with a good share of pain. Today, God has forgiven me for my past sins. Through God's Word, I am learning how to forgive myself for my many mistakes of the past.

PATIENCE IS A VIRTUE

The Bible uses God to illustrate an ultimate example of patience. But neither God, nor His Word needed to show me my dire need for it. My marriage experience taught me a lesson that I'll NEVER forget! Yes, the school of hard knocks taught me that if it takes a lifetime to receive a specific blessing, IT IS BETTER TO PATIENTLY WAIT ON THE LORD, THAN TO TRY TO PRECLAIM YOUR BLESSING OR CLAIM A SUBSTITUTE FOR YOUR ULTIMATE BLESSING. Without further elaboration on this precise statement, I simply PRAY that you take heed to this friendly advice that comes from my heart.

The only other things I want to say regarding patience is that, in addition to learning it through a horrible life experience, I also gained patience through disciplining myself to read the Bible daily.

Patience is necessary because it teaches you to trust and wait on the Lord, and once your prayers or desires are manifested, it increases your faith. Obviously, when you lack patience, you're impulsive. You try to handle life in your own strength; and you generally make a mess of your life---by way of sin.

MY SPIRITUAL JOURNEY THROUGH A MIRROR

Truly, as I took my spiritual journey through the Holy Bible, God placed a mirror on each page for me to reflect on who I was and who I was suppose to be. So, though I read and learned history, I frequently got interrupted by the Holy Spirit, and from time-to-time I asked, "God is that me?!!?" At times my face frowned. Sometimes tears rolled down my cheeks, and on occasion, I smiled. But the bottom line was that God made it clear that this experience wasn't to be associated with some pleasurable novel. I was to grasp the lessons and apply them to my life, and wherever I got stuck or needed help, take it to Christ in prayer. Thus, this mirror had me examining myself and confessing to Christ constantly, "I'm a sinner. . . I'm a sinner. . . Yes, that's me. Lord help." Since I clearly saw sin as an injustice to God, I truly in my heart wanted to be renewed. Did I get stuck along the way? Sometimes I did and other times I didn't.

I NEEDED SELF-CONTROL

As I read the Bible, God taught me, through the Holy Spirit, that I needed to learn greater self-control. Self-control would give me the grace to be more patient and even-tempered. The Bible was very helpful in teaching me self-control because it stressed the importance of "holding the tongue." This valuable lesson was an excellent way to teach me how to mature as a Christian. For example, when Satan comes before you and verbally attacks you, you have three options: (1) You can verbally counterattack, and find yourself arguing and cursing Satan out, so that he can laugh at you and call you a liar and a fake Christian. (2) You can rebuke Satan with Scriptures (but you can't do this until you first learn them). OR (3) you can hold your tongue! This is effective because Satan can't argue by himself. But this does require self-control.

I give God all the glory, because even though I have not gained perfect self-control, I have grown tremendously in this area. The Scriptures showed me that my marriage was built with "cheap" materials, and when anything is built with poor quality materials, it must either be rebuilt or burned down. Rebuilding requires the involved parties to willingly invest whatever it takes and trust God to do the actual reconstruction. Unwillingness on anyone's part means the job won't get done.

In any event, God blessed me with self-control, which gave me grace to sit still in the midst of fiery occasions. For example, there were times when my character was wrongfully attacked, and at those precise moments, I wanted to ignite the house with an atomic explosive! But I knew that if I vented my rage in this manner, no one would escape. So I went to God in prayer, and asked for mercy, guidance, and protection from such attacks.

This was quite an exercise in self-control. I had to hold my tongue and turn my marriage over to God. Quite honestly, it was one of the hardest things I ever had to do in life. Still, patience was the awesome lesson I learned. As a result, my daily routine became, "Say a kind word or be silent and surrender to God. . .kind words or silence, and God."

In light of this, self-control enables you to go to God in times of crisis. When you keep Him in the center of your life, whether you're confessing feelings to Him or crying out His name for mercy---as long as you keep your eyes on Him, NOTHING BUT GOODNESS PREVAILS.

One of the greatest lessons I learned from ALL of these experiences is that half of your Christian life is spent recovering from choices you made when Christ wasn't in the center of your life, and you were lost in sin. God loves you and forgives you. But YOU reap what YOU sow. Obedience to God's Word helps you get through your trials, and leads you to the ultimate blessings that God previously laid out for you in His masterplan. So, as I said before, IF IT TAKES A LIFETIME to receive your blessings, be it a husband, a wife, or a job---IT IS BETTER TO PATIENTLY WAIT ON THE LORD.

CLINGING TO FALSE GODS

Although some lessons were rough, others came easier and faster. Specifically, God showed me that I was worshipping false gods. Needless to say, I was again shocked to learn this revelation! First of all, let me say that the Bible teaches that a false god is ANYTHING placed above God for your guidance, rulership, or comfort. For example, if you're a workaholic, work is your god. If you're happy with money, and sad without it, then money is your god. If you're dependent on drugs, or you're governed by an ungodly mate, or you're hooked to the psychic hotlines---you're in bondage to something other than Christ.

My offenses consisted of consulting Horoscopes, psychic hotlines, dream dictionaries, numerology charts, and blatantly clinging to the prospects of a new and better husband for consolation of my miseries. The problems were: There's ONLY ONE GOD! He created the universe. He is the one and only TRUE COMFORTER; and He alone, is all-knowing---especially since the Scriptures clearly tell you that ANYTHING you want to know, ask in His name, and it will be made known to you. Thus, there was no reason for me to offend God, by consulting false, inaccurate sources, when He is THE SOURCE. There was no need for me to allow a lack of money to steal my joy. And it was unfair for me to get comfort from the thoughts of my future husband, when God had brought me to where I am today! Since Jesus Christ died for me, there was NO ONE on earth that would EVER be able to love me as my Heavenly Father! My actions must have deeply hurt God.

As I read the books of the Bible that dealt with false gods, and understood the meaning of idol worship, I immediately STOPPED reading the horoscopes, discarded my dream books and numerology books. Unfortunately, my release of past regrets, and my firm grip on my hopes for the future took a lot more time. I did, however, learn that the longer it takes you to grow through a lesson, the more it hinders your full blessings that God has in store for you. I can witness that when you surrender to God, blessings follow, because God blessed me immediately after I discarded my evil books. He showed me that I could rely solely on Him, and He gave me answers to questions, even before I asked them. For example, God began speaking to me in my dreams, awakening me, and interpreting them. I recorded the messages in my journal, and have watched some of them manifest. More than that, God foretold me about this book, and gave me an awesome business plan for my future! God is so faithful and good.

If you began to build a personal relationship with God, and you become in-tuned to your Holy Spirit, the only comment I want to make is that you BEWARE of Satan's subtlety. He'll slip false messages into your ear to bring you confusion and doubt. Take precautions by testing all messages with prayer and Scriptures. Seek confirmation from God; and ask yourself if the message, in fact, glorifies God or does it go against His laws.

I don't know how to fully express all that I've learned , and how much I've grown emotionally and spiritually since I've read the Bible from cover-to-cover. I've mentioned how God showed me my temperment, and taught me how to use self-control to handle it, and to use my spiritual gift to vent it. God showed me my selfishness and had me to make a conscious effort to open up and reach out to my friends and loved ones. God blessed me with enough grace to sustain me through a stormy marriage. He had me destroy evil books. He taught me the importance of forgiving anyone who offended me, as well as my need to forgive myself for mistakes I've made. He's blessed me with more patience than I had yesterday; and He's gradually teaching me to rest totally in Him, because He is my only TRUE COMFORTER. Have I arisen to a "point of no return?" Absolutely not! I simple read, gained wisdom, grew spiritually, learned about our Creator, and fell in love with Him. Then I was inspired by God to share my discoveries with the world, in deep hopes that they would be motivated enough to want to read God's Word for themself.

BUILD A PERSONAL RELATIONSHIP

God's Word is a way of life and a day-by-day process. For example, you must read Scriptures daily, obey God's Word, stay in communion with God through prayer, and COUNT YOUR BLESSINGS EVERYDAY. You cannot truely build a personal relationship until you RECOGNIZE GOD'S PRESENCE IN YOUR LIFE. Instead of taking your blessings for granted, you must count them. This acknowledges

God's presence and increases your faith in Him and His promises. I suggest you invest in a notebook, and each day, list everything you have to be thankful for. Remember your eyesight, sane mind, food and shelter! This list should not only have you saying, "Wow! God is good all the time." But it should also help you to be less ungrateful, by selfishly dwelling on all the things that you want God to do for you!

In general, people have a tendency to NOT pray, NOT read God's Word, and NOT praise Him as He deserves. They simply live in their own understanding; take life for granted, until they fall on their face. Then they cry out to God, and say, "WHY ME?" I simply encourage you to build your relationship before disaster strikes. This is true living.

When I make this suggestion, I'm basing it on experience. You see, the Bible teaches you that sin is bad. But when I reflect on WHY my father left home when I was just 4-years old, and WHY he spent the best years of his life in and out of mental institutions; and when I reflect on my past promiscuity, having a daughter out of wedlock, being a workaholic for years, and being deeply, deeply saddened to the point where I just DIDN'T WANT TO GO ON--even trying to kill myself. . . I'm a witness to just how bad sin is. Yes, I was saddened by man's disobedience to God when I read the Bible. But when I looked at MY LIFE, I saw at the root of all my suffering---sin. And I said, "Lord, I don't want no parts of it!"

I thank my Heavenly Father EVERYDAY for loving me enough to save me. He had mercy on me, and I cling to Him and His Word for dear life. Sometimes I think of God's goodness, and it just inspires me to write poems. Two of which come to mind are as follows:

CHECKING IN
From time-to-time
I look in the mirror
I smile because I'm awestruck.
I can't believe it!
Yes, Jesus loves me!
Oh, what a wonderful feeling.

I'm amazed when I look in the mirror
because I see blemishes
I see inconsistencies, mood swings,
imperfect strength and confidence.
I say, "Father, I'm so undeserving."
Then I demand--"I'm NOT WORTHY of your Heavenly Love!"

Then I gaze at the mirror
I'm silent
I stare for a long time

I think how blessed I am!
I'm so grateful.
A tear of joy rolls down my cheek,
Then another.
I'm speechless
I fall to the ground
I weep in deep gratitude
And at the top of my lungs
I scream in the highest alto
THANK YOU JESUS!!!
Then I whisper, Lord Thanks
Thank you, Father...Lord Thanks.
Thank you, Father...thank you...thank you...and more thanks.

LIFE IN ITS FULLEST

Lord, for one moment I saw myself standing
in the green grass barefooted.
And the sun was bright, and the sky was so blue!
I couldn't stop laughing.
You tickled my fancy with joy!
I had all the desires of my heart.
I was a millionaire
But my wealth was YOU and more of YOU!
You were all in my fingertips
And I couldn't have slipped if I wanted to.
It was ecstacy. . .
Father God, you were in my veins, in my heart,
my blood, my hair, my eyes.
You were so filling and uplifting.

WE just CAN'T CONCEIVE ALL THAT YOU ARE AND YOUR JOY.
Once we conceive some of it, our confidence level increases.
We start to smile more. We cry tears of joy
We laugh and we can't stop.

I stood in the park filled with joy
And you set before me---a knight
And he wore shining armour.
He lifted me so high,
gently twirled me around
kissed my hand and chuckled.
But it was the first time in life that he ever laughed!
And he laughed so hard
And it was like music to my ears.
I enjoyed the music so much

til I began to join him in song.

We were both laughing
then came tears of joy
And all we could do was sit on the grass
stare into each others' eyes
And after long moments of silence
we said at the SAME EXACT TIME,
GOD IS SO AWESOME!
I've experienced childbearing and I've witnessed the miracle of child-
birth
And it blew my mind.
But this is different
And it too has BLOWN MY MIND.

IS SATAN KEEPING YOU?

Since I am writing this book in the hopes that you will be inspired,
I sincerely hope that at no given time, I conveyed forcefulness. If you
received a sense of force, it was certainly not my intent. It is unnecessary to force God and His Word on anyone, because you either want
it or you don't. In addition, force is NOT God's way. He truely wants
you to freely choose Him over evil.

Still, I can't resist shedding light on three (3) critical reasons why
many people don't read the Bible. I just believe in my heart that giving
these possibilities is in all due fairness to you, because you may very
well be bound by Satan's tools. The (3) tools which Satan uses to
keep you from the Word of God are: (1) Too much "education", (2)
Fear, and oddly enough (3) racism.

You probably didn't think it was possible to become too "educated." But when you get a certain amount of "knowledge" in you, and
EVERYTHING must be logically proven in order for it to be so, I say
you're too "educated." See, the Word of God is beyond reasoning! It's
spiritual, and if you can't conceive the Spirit of God, yet you have all
the degrees in the world---YOU KNOW NOTHING. My intentions are
not to offend you, but to inform you of the existence of heaven and
hell; and if you cling to your degrees alone, they will earn you a lot of
money and lead you straight to hell. My only advice is that you ask
yourself if you think you have all the answers to life that you need.
Also, ask yourself if your education is blocking your ability to get to
know God or accept Jesus Christ as your Lord and Savior.

The second tool that Satan uses to keep you from reading the
Bible is FEAR. People fear the Bible being bigger than them. They fear
not understanding it. And they fear being convicted on how bad they
are. But if this is of any consolation, that is the whole purpose of
God's laws anyway! They are in the book to show you how bad you

are and how much you need Jesus Christ to save you.

The important lesson to learn is that fear is Satan's subtle way of keeping God's children from reaping their full blessings. For example, suppose that you were destined to fly around the world, teaching and training children for a Home Bible Study Program. This would be an awesome blessing, because you'd be planting seeds in youths, who are NOT so far gone, and they would be learning about Christ BEFORE making a mess of their lives. But, your fear of flying kept you limited to traveling local highways. Although you may have been destined to be rich, through serving the Lord, Satan used your fear to keep you bound and rob you of your ultimate blessing---not to mention the souls that might have been saved through your ministry!

Another example of how fear robs you of your ultimate blessings is that God-ordained marriages are said to be the next best thing to heaven. Yet, fear of commitment and fear of failure keeps so many men and women having sex without marriage; having children out of wedlock; living with partners outside of marriage; and ultimately being robbed of total peace and joy. Satan is fully satisfied as you cling to your fears.

The final tool which Satan uses to keep multitudes of people from God's Word is racism! With this tactic, Satan is very crafty. On that note, I want to say that there are religious groups---one in particular, that insists the Bible is totally inaccurate, right down to Jesus Christ being a black man! It's been historically documented that Jesus was a Jew. But ANY man who reads Revelations 1:14-18, and all they can gather is the ethnicity of Christ---Satan has a serious hold on them!

First of all, the book of Revelations deals with what lies ahead in the future. Satan and Christ, good and evil, and heaven and hell are the dominating themes. And the bottom line is that man should turn from his wicked ways BEFORE the end of time, so that he can have everlasting life! As race is NEVER mentioned, I'm afraid to ask how the subject came into play. And actually, the answer is obvious.

With regards to the physical description of Christ, couldn't His "wooly white hair" be symbolic of the gentleness and innocence of a slain lamb? And with regards to His "feet like unto fine brass..." couldn't that suggest His awesomeness? But without further trying to rectify the thoughts of a fool, I must say that if you are so racist, that Satan used it to blind you of a main, very critical point---you have a problem. Christ is above all races. And the purpose of His voice and vision is to encourage you to foresake evil now, so that you can see the awesome glory of Christ in the afterlife!

On that note, the essence of the Bible is that your spirit is the most important part of you, and God, a spirit, is the Supreme Being of the world. Man needs God, the Father, and His Son, Christ, to save him from damnation and destruction. Man is either good by the grace of God or enslaved to sin.

Education, fear, and racism have no place in the Word of God. Still, in the final analysis, you will choose whether or not you want to be part of it or you don't.

CHOOSING CHRIST

I just want to close this chapter in saying that I'm SO glad I want to be of it---God's Word. As I made my transition from corporate America into research, I knew I would have to make some sacrifices. They included selling my brand new 3-bedroom, 1-car garage rancher, that I purchased at just age 22. I lost my car, and I gave up my luxury of taking annual vacations to beautiful islands. But I had to do it, because during four years of working in corporate America, my soul was screaming at me each day of my life, "YOU DON'T BELONG HERE!!" There was something else that I was suppose to be doing. My spirit weeped profusely because I was doing something that served NO PURPOSE. Anyway, this agony led me into research. I started out doing entrepreneurial studies, and the only thing I want to say about this new position was that I learned that I could very effectively stand before large audiences and give 3-hour seminars. I learned that I absolutely LOVE serving the public. And I just became a glutton and a fanatic for collecting useful information and passing it along.

Did I earn a lot of money or job security doing research? Absolutely not! But did I have a sense of purpose and fulfillment from my life's work? Absolutely! Anyway, the entrepreneurial studies led me to marketing research contracts for universities and major companies. My work was fun, dangerous at times, but very hectic.

In the end, I found myself grossly neglecting my family---leaving my 2-month old son for 9-days, while I trained to manage a research firm; leaving my sick 10-year old daughter to care for herself, while I worked 72-80 hours per week easily. I literally gave my blood, sweat, mind, body, and soul to this project. But I failed because I wasn't willing to stroke my "superiors" ego, by bowing down to them, and rolling out a red carpet when they appeared. My mind and heart told me that my honesty and committment was enough! Unfortunately, it wasn't. And the color of my skin was another contributing factor. Without getting elaborate with details, I resigned from the circus-type lifestyle, and shortly after, the company folded. It was a classic example of how a racist society will use someone to set up their operation and when things are rolling smoothly, try to pull the rug from under their feet. Unfortunately, the tactic backfired on them.

As for me, the resignation led me to STOP and REST! For six years, I gained experience, and grew a passion for research. But my body was tired and I needed to rest. It was during this rest period that

I picked up God's Word, and decided that I was gonna read it from cover-to-cover. It was during this phase of relaxation and reading that God set my life's work before me. You see, as I read, I was literally blown away by what I was reading. And I had already had this passion inside of me for sharing VALUABLE information that I gathered. On that note, God told me to share my excitement and His Word with the world. He told me that one-million copies would be distributed! He told me that after this first book, several others would follow, including a newsletter, and that for the rest of my life, I could just relax and write!

Am I rich today? Only in the Lord. I am allowing God to set my pay scale and give me His security. Am I COMPLETELY SATISFIED with EVERY ASPECT of my life? Absolutely not. Am I happy? I have NEVER BEEN HAPPIER IN ALL MY LIFE!

CHAPTER 4

WHAT'S IN THE BIBLE?

Up to now, I've talked about the making of the Bible; it's content being more than just a historical account; King James Version being the best of 32 new translations; and problems facing the Bible. I've also talked about false religions; the spread of Islam; seven reasons why you should read the Bible for yourself; and what the Bible did for me. As I have tried to inform you, inspire you, and motivate you---my prayers as I draw near the end of this book, are that I've stimulated your appetite enough that you will commit to daily reading of God's Word.

As a final attempt to get you stirred up, I'm simply going to give you an overview of each book of the Bible. My hopes are that as you review the general content, your personal needs will be ADDRESSED, and you'll want to have your needs MET by going to the Source itself.

GENESIS

The overall theme of the book of Genesis is **BEGINNINGS**. As you travel through life and experience its trials and tribulations, and you get your share of bumps and bruises---you're bound to ask the question, "What's the point?" You start to wonder, "Why am I here, and why must I continue to suffer?" Genesis brings you to the beginning of time, and in doing so, shows you God's ultimate purpose for all of man.

With regards to the beginning of time, the Bible assumes God's presence. For example, there is never an attempt to prove His existence. God is from everlasting to everlasting, and you must choose to believe this truth or reject it. The triune of God, the Father, His Son, and the Holy Spirit, are also introduced in Genesis 1:26 when God says, "Let US make man in OUR image..." Again, you must accept or not accept the Trinity. Thus, the very first step to entering God's Word is ACCEPTING that there is a God.

Assuming God's existence, Genesis introduces Him as the Creator of the universe. God reveals His perfect plan for man, and man commits his first rebellion against God, which alters His perfect plan. Despite man's fall into sin, God NEVER gives up on him, and that is right from the beginning of time, until the end!

There are seemingly infinite lessons that can be pulled out of the book of Genesis. But if they were all mentioned, what would be the purpose in your reading it for yourself? As such, the intent here is to highlight main ideas.

For example:

.Genesis 1 and 2 teaches that God created the universe by speaking words! 1:3 says, "And God SAID, 'Let there be light.' And there WAS light." Then, 1:6 says, "And God SAID, 'Let there be a firmament in the midst of the waters, and let it divide the waters from the waters.' And God MADE the firmament..." And throughout these two chapters, God SAYS it and creation is DONE. The significance of this illustration is that **God is our creator and there is POWER In HIS WORDS**!

.2:23-25 reveals that **God ordained marriage and sex** from the very beginning, so that man could be fruitful and multiply. Yet man, without God in the center of his life has turned marriage into a hell-haven. Divorce rates are at an all-time high, and sex is no longer sacred. The results is a dysfunctional society at large. The point being, **God has a perfect plan for each of our lives, and we are at liberty of accepting it or rejecting it.**

.Genesis 2:15-20 teaches that **rewards follow work.** Since rewards come AFTER work is done, there seems to be no allowance for gambling at the casinos or playing the lottery. Although gambling, alone, won't keep you from going to heaven, it's caused many people to lose their homes, cars, and entire families. While these particular losses are extreme, and refer to people addicted to gambling, the critical fact to remember is that every addiction starts off as an occasional indulgence. The occasions become frequent, and the frequencies lead to an addiction. The main point is that **the more you live out of God's will, the worse your life becomes.**

.Genesis 1:31 teaches that **God's normal way of working is through a process.** For example, He made everything in six days, even though He is almighty and powerful, and could have made everything in an instance. This process of God's timing is what gives you patience, and builds your faith. As such, Christians become born again in an instance, but inner changes are gradual and the process lasts a lifetime.

.Genesis 3:12-13 shows you man's tendency to shift blame on others, and not take responsibility for his actions. In general, **if people began to take full responsibility for their actions, there would be more productive lives; less resentment and hostility.**

.Genesis 9, through Noah's building of an ark, teaches that **it's to your advantage to obey God**. The more love and faith you have for God, the more you will obey Him, and it is obedience which brings about ultimate blessings.

EXODUS

The theme of the book of Exodus is **EXITS**. This book deals with God rescuing the Israelites from slavery in Egypt; leading them to the Desert of Sinai; and giving Moses the laws to govern them. This book clearly shows you the power of God over evil. But the most delightful thing you should see is that God NEVER FAILS MAN! However, He really does expect for man to trust and obey Him in return for His unfailing mercies.

Other observations to make as you read this book are as follows: .Moses is the main character of the book of Exodus. The extremely valuable lesson that you learn from Moses is that God has a purpose for each of our lives. Sometimes when you get consumed with your self-doubts, you put yourselves at risk of missing out on your blessings. Other times, you just battle with God along the way, as you try to resist your calling! For example, when God chose Moses, Moses doubted his ability to lead (3:11-13). He argued with God that he was unworthy and lacked authority. Moses was also afraid of people not trusting him, and he was insecure about his speech difficulties. In short, Moses fought "tooth and nail" to resist what God had already set out for him to do. As Moses turned out to be one of the most powerful leaders in history, you see that **God is all-knowing, and He really does know what's best.** Through this lesson, Moses offers a marvelous sense of hope to people who have similar self-doubts.

.Exodus 16 teaches that **God will sometimes provide you with bare essentials ONLY to keep you humbly relying on Him,** so that "Ye shall know that I am Lord your God."

.Many people question why the Israelites were God's chosen people. However, God has a right to choose whomever He wants, because He's God! Still, Exodus teaches that **the choosing of the Israelites was strictly an act of God's grace,** because these chosen ones were NOT brave, obedient, impressive or even faithful to God. In essence, they did NOTHING to deserve their priivilege as God's chosen people.
As such, when you are chosen as God's servants, it is NOT because you are special, and it does NOT give you reason to become prideful. **You are also chosen by the grace of God,** and should show gratitude.

.Exodus 20 sums up man's duty to God and his neighbors, through the Ten Commandments. These duties include loving others as you love yourself; worshipping God only; shunning false gods and idols; not using God's name in vain; Sabbath Day being devoted to God; Honoring parents and forbidding adultery to protect the sanctity of family life; forbidding murder, stealing; and bearing false witness and covetousness.

LEVITICUS
The theme of the book of Leviticus is **offerings and feasts**. God set up laws regarding holiness and worship. However, these instructions given to priests, regarding religious ceremonies, peace offerings, rituals for the installation of priests, marriage laws, and keeping every

seventh year as a Sabbatical---all became barriers to God's will. These instructions, intended to govern the life of the Israelites, became barriers because the rules became more important than the meaning behind them.

As with religious people today, the Israelites were so caught up into the rituals of making sacrifices to God, yet their hearts never changed enough for them to receive inner changes. Inner changes would have made it less necessary for so many offerings and sacrifices. As I mentioned earlier, if you step on a person's toe 150 times in a single day, the words, "excuse me" lose their meaning to the victim suffering a sore, aching toe. You must STOP stepping on the victim's toe. As such, you must also STOP SINNING and saying, "ooh, God forgive me."

As God provides a way for atonement, by offering sacrificial blood of Christ, the most important lesson of the book of Leviticus is to show you the need for Jesus Christ. Sacrifices, offerings, vows, and tithes mean NOTHING unless you have a changed heart, and you get this change from Christ. It is your faith in Him that enables Him to make necessary changes in you.

If you lack a loving, caring, selfless spirit, then you need Jesus Christ in your heart, and this is something you should pray for. Sunday worship, serving on the usher board, or singing in the church choir are mere activities in the eyes of God, if your heart is hard, cold, and self-centered.

NUMBERS

The book of Numbers is representative of the **WANDERING** of the Israelites in the wilderness for forty years. Throughout this book, you see the continual faithfulness of God, in spite of the unbelievable sin of man. You see a patient God; an unchanging God, who's true to His Word, as He leads His people through the wilderness and provides for their needs.

You should note that the Israelites were wandering for forty years, in the first place, because of their disobedience and rebellion against God. This historical event is no different from today's society. For example, today many people suffer from regrets, grudges, anger, sadness, and depression. And at the root of it all is rebellion against God's way. Even as we go through our trials, God is with us! Imagine over 4,000 years, and He has NEVER changed. God is good all the time.

DEUTERONOMY

The theme of the book of Deuteronomy is **Second Laws**. The Israelites were previously given the laws of Moses, and they wore the laws on their head (11:18-20). They showed outer signs of being religious. But there was no sign of a personal relationship with God. The purpose of the second laws was to have the laws placed on their hearts. This book teaches that love is what makes the difference. For example, God tells you to love Him with all of your heart. And truly, you CANNOT OBEY GOD without first loving Him. In light of this, love is more than just a feeling. Love is a DECISION to serve another person's interest, and it is ONLY through God's help that this decision can be made with "all thy heart." You must therefore, pray and ask God to teach you how to love Him.

Several other important lessons come through the book of Deuteronomy:

.In Moses' first speech (chapters 1-3), he reviewed Israel's history and how God dealt with them. Moses reminded them that as they grumbled and complained for forty years, God guided them and even delivered them! This is so parallel to today's society. There are people who live through one or maybe even two world wars. They witness many lives lost, and they are bitter that God allowed it to happen. They complain, "there can't POSSIBLY be a God and He allow such catastrophies to take place!" Sadly, these angry people are as blinded as the Israelites. They fail to recognize that out of ALL the dead bodies, God saved them.

Whether you are a prison inmate, or a poverty-stricken, homeless person--IF YOU ARE STILL HERE, you have an opportunity to make today better than yesterday. If you can just RECOGNIZE GOD'S GOODNESS by counting your very life as a blessing, God will guide you through the absolute worst circumstances.

.When man committed his first sin (Genesis 3), Adam blamed Eve, and Eve blamed the Serpent, and neither Adam nor Eve took responsibility for their actions. You see this blame-shifting behavior again in Deuteronomy. The Israelites suffered because of their disobedience to God, but they blamed God for their suffering. Even Moses demonstrated this tendency when he gave his speeches. For example, in Numbers 20, Moses acted out in anger and broke his faith in God, before his followers. This action led to Moses being punished in a way that he would die BEFORE getting to the promised land. In Deuteronomy 3:26 and 4:21, Moses blamed the Israelites for provoking his punishment. Moses did not admit that he lacked enough patience to CONSISTENTLY keep his faith in God. And such is human nature. It's a lot easier to point a finger than to look within yourself and take responsibility for your actions.

.Deuteronomy 13 warned against idolatry, which at the time, largely consisted of the worship of carved images, like the golden calf. However, today you must be conscious that idolatry is NOT limited to carved images. Idolatry is ANYTHING reverenced above God. So you must ask yourself, "What are the priorities or the things which come first in your life?" To answer this question in truth, you should not say what you THINK should be your priorities. Instead answer, what things ACTUALLY dominate your life. For example, you may say that God is first in your life; your family is second priority; and your work is third priority. But in reality, if you are working overtime, neglecting your family, and have no time for God, then your first priority is NOT God.

Your work or money may be your god. If satisfying YOUR DESIRES are priority in your life, then YOU are a god. Money, sex, friends, drugs, coffee, food, cigarettes---whatever governs your life is your god. Deuteronomy 13 warns against idolatry because it is offensive to God. Afterall, He is Creator of the universe; God is your reason for being; and King of Kings. Yet, you reduce Him to less than a cigarette or a bottle of beer! You get lonely or feel defeated and you run past God's Word to grab a mere crutch.

You are fairly warned in God's Word, because the repercussions are severe. That which you reverence above God will surely destroy you by way of cancer, aids, drug addiction, obesity or anxiety. A workaholic will lose his or her family and friends. Living to find a man or woman of your dreams will lead you from one failed relationship to another, NEVER finding satisfaction, because your true NEED is deeper and more complex. Greed for money will cause you to kill your mother or even yourself.

Yet, if God is first in your life, you will get the desires of your heart. God's Word is truely a protective sword. His laws are for your own good and they protect you.

.Many people think that having a relationship with God is close to impossible! They think that God wants them to "ascend to heaven and swim in the sea to meet His commands" (30:11-14). Yet, in Moses closing speech, you learn that what God expects from you is very simple. He wants you to understand, believe and obey His Word.

JOSHUA

After Moses died, Joshua commanded the armies that conquered most of the territory in the promised land. As such, the theme of the book of Joshua is **CONQUERER**. While Exodus, Numbers, and Deuteronomy gives numerous examples of how NOT to be, Joshua offers you a renewed sense of hope! 40 years have passed, and there's a new generation that's decided to trust God no matter what. This trusting attitude is what led the Israelites to their conquering spirit, reflected in 2:24.

Joshua is a wonderful book of hope because it shows you that people CAN follow God's instructions! But more than that, when people follow God's instructions precisely, it elevates their faith to new heights. For example, the Israelites succeeded when they relied on God. Yet, the battle of Ai (7:1-13) and the trick of the Gibeonites (9:14) shows you what happened when the Israelites failed to seek God's will. Thus, this book reinforces earlier advice to PRAY about Everything and OBEY the Holy Spirit.

Other valuable lessons were as follows:
.Joshua had reason to be fearful. He was a new, inexperienced leader called to continue the works of Moses, one of the greatest leaders in history. However, God encouraged him (1:9) to "be strong and of good courage."

.The book of Joshua shows you God's direct involvement in history. In doing so, you should recognize that you CAN trust God to guide your life and KNOW that only good will prevail. However, God is NOT automatically true to His promises. You must fear and serve Him in truth, to reap your blessings.

.For 40 years God miraculously fed the Israelites "manna." Then the food ceased and they had to grow food for themselves. This (5:12) teaches you that God delivers you through your hard times. But once He does, He expects for you to utilize your spiritual gifts to glorify His name and care for yourself in effect. This is critical because there are people who become Christians and suddenly believe that God is going to just take care of them with no strings attached. To your dismay, you don't become Christians so that you can have the luxury of USING God! You are ALL HERE TO SERVE GOD. As such, God saves you so that He can use you to win more souls!

This does not apply to when Christians are in "training" and God has them "sitting at His feet," feeding on His Word, or preparing for a work. If you are destined to be a pastor, a politician, or a teacher, Joshua is an excellent book to study leadership qualities. Joshua was successful because of his ability to follow instructions as well as give them.

JUDGES
As Israel experienced one failure after another, and the Canaanites worshipped everything from the storm god, and the goddess of harvest, to spirits of rivers and hills, the Law of Moses was endangered, and historically documented disasters occured. To combat these problems, God raised leaders called "judges." Since a pattern developed under these judges, the theme of this book is CYCLES.

The cycles which occured then, and now, are that God allows suffering as a consequence for disobedience. When things get really rough, you call on God. He rescues you. Shortly after, you forget your need for Him, then you fall again. And this vicious CYCLE repeats itself.

The most important lessons from this book are as follows:
.The wages of sin is death, and SIN is SIN, whether it's the sophisiticated sin of a king or the barbaric sin of a peasant or even stealing a nickel! Judges shows you that when people do their own thing, chaos and destruction results. And when there's chaos, there's trickery, deception, no fairness, or justice.

.Most of the judges were flawed. For example, Samson (chapters 14-16) was extremely vunerable to his lust for women. Gideon (7:15) won a battle and then led the Israelites into idolatry. Jephthah (chapters 11-12) was a former outlaw and knew very little about the God he was suppose to serve. Abimelech (chaptes 9-10) slaughtered 70 half brothers so that he could become a king. And Jephthah and Gideon killed fellow Israelites who failed to support them. What should these examples teach you? We are all flawed because we are ALL sinners, and NOT ONE man is perfect. As such, these ugly faces of "leaders" should encourage you to strive for perfection, but RECOGNIZE that God can use you, even in your imperfect state!

It's easy enough to look at your present state and think, "God can't possibly use me! My life is a mess." But truly, He goes after the worst of us! Afterall, what testimonies can a saint give unless they've experienced an abortion, homelessness, poverty, killing or being a victim of a crime? In essence, you CANNOT inspire a lost soul unless you have, yourself, been lost and delivered from the bondage of sin.

RUTH

The theme of this 4-chapter book, which can be read in one day is LOVE STORY. Ruth tells the story of two widows who lost everything when their husbands died. A deep friendship formed between the two, and the poor women found help through the grace of God.

In this short book, you learn that even in times of crisis, you can stilll live according to the laws of God, and when you do, God blesses you abundantly.

.As the loyalty and love of the two friends survived the suffering, you should learn that love is longsuffering. Regarding male-female relationships, anyone can "love" through good times, gory romance, or steamy sex. But that which lasts through hard times is strengthened and becomes everlasting love. Such is also the case with friendships. ANYONE can use the term "friend" in good times. But hardships will unveil your true friends, if any exists.

1SAMUEL

Samuel was a leader between the era of the judges and the

kings, and he appointed Israel's first king, Saul. As such, **Saul** is the theme of this book. Samuel failed as king and then tried to prevent God's chosen one, King David from taking the throne.

.Chapters 1 and 2 teach you that from bitter pain comes great promises---if your pain leads you to God.

.The overall message of this book is that God does NOT make His people immune to the changes of human life. He just gives them the grace to see things to a satisfactory end. It is a gross misconception to think that because you become a Christian and read the Bible, you'll get immunity to life's ups and downs. Suffering is a part of life.

.As you read this book, note that God chooses His own leaders. For example (2:12-26) the corrupt sons of Eli were SUPPOSE to become the nations' leaders. But because they didn't know God, God chose Samuel. Samuel annointed Saul, but when Saul failed to honor God, he lost his authority. David preceded Saul.

2SAMUEL

1Samuel told of David's youth and exile. 2Samuel focused on David's leadership as a king. As such, the theme of 2Samuel was DAVID. David played the harp, wrote poems, fought battles, faked insanity, rejoiced in the Lord, lusted after Bathsheba, and committed murder and adultery. Through it all, David was the greatest king in Israel's history.

The good and evil examples of David's life teach you not to put too much trust in man. But in witnessing David's victories, you also see what God can do with someone who totally trusts in Him. God favored David because David took full responsibility for his mistakes. He was willing to repent and start over again, no matter how far off base he went.

Another good quality that David possessed was his humbleness to God. David never forgot his beginning as a mere shepherd; that he held his powerful position by the grace of God; and that God had a right to take away his power at any given time. David's humbleness was important because there are many people that go through life, angry and bitter, feeling like the world owes them something. Through David, you learn that NO ONE, including God owes you NOTHING. Once you grasp this concept, humbleness will keep you in a more thankful, praiseful state of mind. When you praise God, you also serve Him more diligently.

Important lessons of this book are as follows:
.Through the Philistine's defeat (5:19), you should learn that you can safely rely on God to fight ALL of your battles for you. The only obsta-

cle before you is, "DO YOU trust God enough to let Him lead you to victory?"

.Although David was a magnificent leader, his shortcomings did not get overlooked by God. Chapters 11-20 show you the "cancerous" results of David's private sins and poor family leadership. For example, his son Amnon raped his sister Tamar, and Absalom killed his brother Amnon in revenge. David sinned by sleeping with Bathsheba while she was married, and the result of his own immoral behavior kept him from properly disciplining his children. The most important lesson from these chapters is that NO ONE ESCAPES the wages of sin.

.Remember that ONE SIN is like a locust. For example, David lusted for Bathsheba. Then he slept with her and got her pregnant while she was married. Bathsheba's husband, Uriah was killed in an effort to keep the pregnancy a secret. David's family was neglected because his focus was NOT evenly divided among righteousness. And it ALL began with the sin of lust! One sin killed and destroyed many!

1 KINGS
SOLOMON is the theme of the book of 1Kings, since he succeeded David. When Solomon died, a civil war broke out that destroyed Israel, and a series of mostly bad kings followed him.

The first half of 1Kings describes Solomon's life as it was handed to him from his father, King David and his mother, Queen Bathsheba. As God blessed Solomon with the gift of wisdom, Solomon became the richest and wisest man in the world. He gained great respect and success; and his greatest accomplishment was the building of God's temple.

The second half of this book presents the fall of Israel from its very prosperous era. Solomon filled his life with luxuries and as he did, he moved further and further away from that which was MOST important---Christ. As you read, note how Solomon's love for luxury turned to greed, and how this greed led him to 700 wives and 300 concubines! In an effort to try to please 700 foreign wives, Solomon had altars built for each of their gods.

Other lessons you should learn are:
.The sin of greed leads to chaos and confusion, because as your life increases with worldly possessions, you get consumed with trying to maintain "things" and you grow away from what's really important. In the end, Solomon had to acknowledge that fearing God is the beginning of wisdom, and a true dream house is built on the wisdom of God.

.It is NOT God's will that any man be poverty-stricken. However, God shows you through Solomon, what TYPICALLY happens to man when he achieves wealth. Unless you have the wisdom of God and have Him as first in your life, wealth blinds you into foolishly thinking that you have EVERYTHING YOU NEED when you're rich. But in reality, everything you have can be lost. As such, Jesus Christ is your only true security. So if you are rich, you should pray for the wisdom of God.

.Solomon made many mistakes as a leader. But his biggest was (11:6) "Solomon did evil in the sight of the Lord, and went not fully after the Lord, as did David, his father." Solomon got so consumed with his greed that he failed to make God the center of his life. Whereas Israel once worshipped God, they shifted to the worship of many gods. The result was a fallen nation. Today, when God is not the center of your life, you generally make a mess of it.

2 KINGS
The theme of 2 Kings is **EXILE**. This book continues to give a record of the kings of the divided nation. None of the northern kings consistently followed God. As a result, Israel was destroyed by an invader. Babylon conquered the southern part of the nation, Judah, and the Israelites went into exile.

2 Kings ends with a very grim picture of Jerusalem destroyed; the Israelites enslaved; and God's temple ruined---all because of the constant ruling of kings without relying on God for guidance, and the widespread of idolatry (17:16-18).

Although God has been in control throughout history, rulers have thought that they were in control. You should learn from this book that sin brings judgment on people, and righteousness brings God's blessings. You should also notice that God's mercies endure forever, and that He remains fair and just. For example, God NEVER sends judgment without first sending a warning (through His prophets).

1 CHRONICLES
The theme of 1 Chronicles is **EDITORIAL DAVID**. This book begins with a complete genealogical record of Israel back to Adam. The first nine chapters recapture the Israelites' history and family tree. The many names are mentioned to show you that God forgets no one. This is valuable to remember when you're going through trials, and you feel alone, like God has forgotten you.

The remaining chapters 10 to 29 retells the story of David, focusing on all the good that he left for future generations. The purpose of omitting David's weaknesses was to stress the importance of worshipping God. You also shouldn't miss the positive effects on a nation that's led by a man who relies on God for guidance.

Despite Israel's bloody history, 22:8-9 teaches you that God does NOT favor war. David was directed to conduct some wars out of necessity to regain order. However, war is not God's ideal solution. He is holy. This is made apparent in God not wanting His temple "rebuilt by a man of war." Thus, there's a time and a place for everything, and though it is NEVER in God's will that man should sin, sometimes sin is allowed. Your protection comes from praying on all of your life choices and waiting for an answer from God. (Still, all sin brings about judgment.)

2 CHRONICLES

2 Chronicles records the history of rulers in Judah, with emphasis on the good kings. As such, the theme of this book is **JUDAH**. This book primarily gives a historical account of Judah, stressing the glory of Solomon's reign, the glory of the temple, and the overall victories of Israel. The purpose of this positive account was to offer the Israelites a renewed sense of hope.

In reviewing Judah's history, you should see a definite pattern of righteous kings being rewarded and blessed, and evil kings being punished. This lesson reminds you that God was as much in charge then as He is today, and will be in the future. Again, see that EVERY SIN IS JUDGED.

EZRA

Ezra was a great Jewish leader who led the Israelites to Palestine after their captivity in Bablyon. The book of Ezra shows you how God judged His people for their sins, but NEVER stopped loving them. For example, He kept His promise by bringing the Israelites back home, and never abandoning them. Both then and now, God expects your worship in return for His love. As such, the theme of the book of Ezra is **TEMPLE and PEOPLE**.

God expressed His desire for our worship when He sent the prophets Haggai and Zechariah to speed up the rebuilding of the temple (chapters 5, 6).

Important lessons you should gain from this book are:

.If God gives you work to do, recognize Satan and his adversaries will do everything in their powers to stop you. Chapter 4 describes three (3) different tricks Satan will use to hinder you from doing God's work. For example, (4:1-3) your opponents will try to offer you "help" that will lead to compromises or a takeover by nonbelievers. (4:45) Your opponents may try to discourage you, frighten you, or just frustrate you. Finally, (4:23-24) your opponents may try to use power to force you to stop God's work. The major point here is to stay focused on whatever

God sets before you, because Satan is busy.

NEHEMIAH

As the book of Nehemiah began with his inspection of the walls, and the rebuilding of the Tabernacle, the theme of this book is **WALLS**. Walls are necessary for protection. Walls enable you to separate yourself from non-believers so that your strength in the lord can increase by way of fasting, confessing your sins, reading God's Word, and worshipping and praising Him (9:1-5).

The most important lesson you should learn from this book, is how to pray. Nehemiah teaches you to pray diligently by first going to God confessing your sins and weaknesses. This keeps a respect for God and His Word, because your admission of your sins is a way of saying, "I know what you expect of me, and I've failed to obey you perfectly." At this point, you should be sorry in your heart. Then you can pray for forgiveness and ask God to have mercy on you. Once you have confessed your sins and asked for forgiveness, then you can REMIND God of His promises to YOU and put in your prayer requests. Your prayers should also consist of thanking and praising God for all that He has done for you.

Nehemiah demonstrated this manner of praying, and it's effective because it reminds YOU that God comes first, BEFORE your prayers can be answered. A final point you should learn is that prayer and action goes hand-in-hand. For example, you can pray for wealth until the skies fall down. But unless you put forth effort and work, you'll simply be uttering words.

ESTHER

The theme of the book of Esther is **Queen of Persia**. It's a story about a plot to destroy the Jews, after Persia destroyed Babylon, and the Jews were still in captive in Persia. In a twist of events, "Esther" altered the plans and the Jews were saved from extermination.

The underlying message is that God protects His people even in their captivity, and He works ALL things together for the good. You should also see how God uses people to accomplish His purpose. Although God is never specifically mentioned in the book of Esther, He is always present. And the implication is that He takes care of ALL people, whether they are Christians or non-believers.

CHAPTER 5

THE END OF HISTORY — FIVE BOOKS OF POETRY

JOB

The theme of the book of Job is **God's SOVEREIGNTY**. This long dramatic poem is about a perfectly uprighteous, God-fearing man who one day lost his family, his wealth, and his health. He then wished he was dead. Job's friends tried to comfort him by offering their advice.

One of Job's friends suggested that he was just being corrected by God and all would be well in the end. Another one of Job's friends suggested that either Job or his family must have sinned because God is just and God would not have punished him for no reason. To this response, Job knew that he wasn't perfect. But he saw a complete imbalance between what he did and how he was "punished." Finally, Job's other friend suggested that God restores you when you put aside your wickedness. However, Job didn't accept these accusations, because he saw the oppression of the poor, and evil around the world going unpunished, and even the wicked people prospering. Thus, all of these suggestions were fallacies and suffering remained a mystery.

The underlying question of this book is why there is so much sin and suffering if there's an almighty God who's powerful enough to do something about it? In the end of the poem God speaks to Job himself. Since Job was not a rebel, he submitted to the wisdom of God. He realized that you don't need "answers" to life's problems as much as you need God himself.

Although many people talk about the tragedies of Job, few stress the end of this lovely poem (42:10). Not only was Job's health restored, but God blessed him with TWICE as much wealth as he lost! The valuable lessons that you should get from this book are: (1) Man, made from dust, has no right to question God. (2) Man needs to trust in God, because he simply doesn't have enough knowledge to understand why things happen as they do. (3) It is possible to rise above your circumstances, by faith in God, because He knows why everything happens and works good for those who love Him. (4) When you have NOTHING but God, GOD IS ENOUGH. (5) Finally, God does NOT cause sin and suffering. Satan attacks you and tries to tempt you, in an effort to get your focus off of God. You pass the test if you grow stronger in the Lord, as a result of your suffering. If you get discouraged or angry with God and curse Him, Satan wins you back from God. Then your life generally goes from bad to worse.

PSALMS

The theme of the book of Psalms is **PRAISE and WORSHIP**. The book consists of prayers and hymns, covering all of the human emotions; and they teach you how to relate to God. You should also learn that God has a personal concern for you, and He wants you to come to Him, JUST AS YOU ARE! You should, finally, learn that whether you feel joy, sorrow, anger or doubt, whatever you've done, and wherever you are, if you OFFER yourself to God, He helps you and gives you the strength to live again. Because God is almighty and powerful, He can help you when you turn to Him for deliverance! This is one of the most inspirational books of the Bible.

The subjects of the 150 chapters are as follows:

CHAPTER	SUBJECT
1	The way of the righteous
2	The king's triumph
3	Confidence facing the enemy
4	Thoughts in the night
5	A morning prayer
6	Prayer for mercy
7	Prayer of a wronged man
8	God's glory and man's honor
9	Praise to God
10	God hears and acts
11	The Lord our refuge
12	Good thoughts for bad times
13	The deserted soul
14	Fate of a fool
15	Happiness of the holy
16	Joy in God's presence
17	Deliverance from the wicked
18	Calling upon God in distress
19	Works and Word of God
20	Prayer for the King
21	Success of a king
22	Cry of anguish, song of praise
23	Shepherd Psalm
24	Song of the King of glory
25	Prayer for guidance and protection
26	Basis of judgment
27	David's song of confidence
28	Prayer for help
29	Lord of the thunderstorm
30	Lord my helper
31	My timing is in God's hands
32	Prayer during distress
33	The Lord provides and delivers
34	Praise and Trust
35	Plea for judgment
36	Wickedness confronting God's love'
37	Blessings to the righteous

PROVERBS

The theme of the awesome, down-to-earth book of Proverbs is **WISDOM**. Proverbs consist of basic instructions and advice on EVERY aspect of life to lead you to a successful, fulfilled life. This book teaches you that your first step to wisdom is to trust and respect God. Moreover, a man is NEVER truly wise unless he trusts in God, because all the intellect without humility in the presence of God and a willingness to learn from Him, will lead man astray. Since everything that pertains to a successful living is a concern to God, and He's made provisions for it, you must be willing to learn from the ultimate Teacher---God, Himself.

Proverbs unveils dangerous inner attitudes, such as anger, pride, jealousy, fear of people, and conceit. Since these qualities are often present in you, being aware of them helps you to confront them, and in the interim, begins your personal growth.

One of the very valuable lessons that Proverbs teach is the distinction of three problem people that you should avoid. This is important because often times, you may find yourself transgressing, and at the root of it is the company you're keeping. Thus, Proverbs 1:22 warns you against three problem people: "Simple ones," "scorners," and "fools."

"Simple ones" are the least harmful people, because they simply live without thinking, and they're just too lazy to change. The threat to you is your personal growth being stunted by stagnant people NOT seeking the Lord. "Fools" have a good sense of right and wrong, truth and fallacy. They've just made a conscious decision to live by their own understanding, independent of God and independent of God's advice. Obviously, keeping the company of fools increases your chances of becoming one. "Scorners" are the most dangerous of all because they are actually rebels against God. They make their prideful position known to everyone. Obviously, if you are in the presence of people who stand up to God, and challenge the Almighty, you are not being taught or encouraged to fear Him.

As this lesson teaches you how to see people with more discernment, the main idea is: if you want to be rich, you can't make progress by staying in the company of poor people. If you want to be happy, you can't stay in the presence of sad or miserable people. If you want to be healthy, you can't dwell in the presence of sickly, diseased, or contagious people---be it physical, mental, emotional, or spiritual. But MOST IMPORTANT, if you want to grow in the Lord, you can't stay amongst non-believers.

ECCLESIASTES

The theme of the book of Ecclesiastes is **VANITY and EMPTI-NESS.** Whether you are wise or a fool, you must die. As such, wealth, wisdom, fame, and pleasure ALL mean absolutely NOTHING, if you don't have God in your life.

This book teaches that if you try to live for SELF and please self only, without considering the needs of others or God, your life will be wasted, and leave you feeling empty. Although this book may seem grim, as it denounces wealth, wisdom, and pleasure, truly, it says that you CAN and SHOULD ENJOY LIFE! You just need to enjoy life by putting God first. You need to remember that because you must account to God for everything you do, there's NO PERFECT TIME to surrender your life to Him. Give your life to God today!

SONG OF SOLOMON

The theme of the book of Song of Solomon is **LOVE in MAR-RIAGE.** This romantic poem teaches you how love is meant to be. God values love between a man and a woman, and in fact, ordained love and marriage as a good and holy way to stay in obedience to His laws. As such, this book is appropriately placed in the Bible.

Song of Solomon describes the longing of two lovers for one another (chapters 2-4); the struggles that they have to overcome (chapter 5); and the joy that lovers find in being together. The love is without shame. The feelings are mutually filled with delight, and they are natural.

The love described in this book SYMBOLIZES God's love for Israel and the love of Jesus Christ for His church. Because love is so wonderful, you learn in 3:5 that it should NEVER be rushed. In addition, because love takes control of your life, "as it is as strong as death" (8:6), you must treat love with caution and respect.

This poem gives new meaning to love! Love heals. It makes flowers grow. It's equal. It's romantic, exciting, and NOTHING LESS than a gift of God, from God. Although Song of Solomon is a delight and breathtaking, it also offers a very serious message. Spousal abuse is

NOT love. Cruelty, abandonment, and jealousy is NOT love. Encouraging a partner to engage in dangerous activities such as taking drugs or having unsafe sex is NOT love. Therefore, be encouraged to shy away from "things" other than that which is described in this book. Love is not sex or lust. Love is obedience, longsuffering, unconditional, patience, caring, kindness in words and deeds, fearless, deep, and lasting.

CHAPTER 6

BOOKS OF THE PROPHETS

ISAIAH

The theme of the book of Isaiah is **GROAN and GLORY**. Isaiah looked at the failures of Israel, Judah, Assyria, Palestine, Moab, Damascus, Ethiopia, Egypt, Babylon, Tyre, and Ephraim, and pointed to the coming of Messiah to bring about peace.

As this book is one of the largest books of the Bible, many lessons come through. For example, God freely forgives everyone who turns to Him in repentence and faith. This means whether you're a child molester, rapist, mass murderer, or simply a liar and a cheat, God NEVER changes. To Him, sin is sin. It's all offensive and it ALL leads to death. As such, if you recognize your sinful state, and truly are sorry in your heart, and you truly want to change for the better, God forgives you!

Although God is seen as Savior in this book, and He redeems His people from captivity, the message is clear in chapters 4, 7:14, and 9:16, that God is sending His Servant in the future, to bear the sins of everyone.

Satan is again introduced in 14:12-20, and it's here that you should recognize that Satan wants the power of God. He wants everyone to worship him instead of God. Satan is greedy and he wants it all! This is a very critical revelation, because if you can conceive the depths of this desire, then you'll better understand that Satan uses EVERY trick in the book to win people's souls.

Satan usually keeps you bound by your weaknesses. For example, if you are consumed by underlying fears, or guilt, love of sex and money, or anger, or jealousy---WHATEVER qualities keep you from diligently seeking after Jesus Christ, you are bound! Your bondage is the very thing that can lead you straight to hell, because it keeps you from TRULY ACCEPTING CHRIST, and allowing the Holy Spirit to transform you into the likeness of God. As I said before, if you can at least recognize Satan's main objective, then you may look at your weaknesses in a new light.

The fact that Isaiah often delivered bad news, and was deeply saddened by the news he delivered (16:9) teaches you that when God has a calling on your life, and He gives you a job, it is NOT always pleasant. First of all, since nobody likes to deal with the truth, there's discomfort in that aspect of the job in itself. Still, you must remember to keep your eyes on God and recognize that you are doing a work of the Lord. Thus, the pain that "YOU" bring forth (in speaking the truth) is really for cleansing purposes, and NOT meant to intentionally harm for the sake of evilness.

Another factor which can make a job uncomfortable is rejection. Unfortunately, God does NOT promise ANYONE an easy ride through life. Just because He gives you a job does NOT mean the job will be well received by family members, friends, and the public at large. You may be laughed at, ridiculed, persecuted, or just outwardly rejected. Through this discomfort, you become stronger in the Lord. Don't get discouraged because God promises you peace and joy. Therefore, as you grow and live for the Lord, you learn to also rest in Him.

The hope of the book of Isaiah is the future, which is Jesus Christ, freedom from sin, and everlasting life. Chapter 55, invites EVERYONE to partake in this gift of eternity, and chapter 56 reinforces that salvation is for everyone. You need only to want it and choose it over death.

JEREMIAH

The theme of the book of Jeremiah is **REPENTANCE**. God chose Jeremiah to be "over the nations...and kingdoms...to build, and to plant." In all of these responsibilities, his only resource was his mouth! Jeremiah wanted out of his job (chapter 1, 20:9) because he had to give warnings to government officials (chapter 22), and they hated hearing the messages. Jeremiah was arrested and imprisoned several times (chapter 26), and almost killed. Although Jeremiah remained obedient, no prophet exposed his feelings to God like he did. Jeremiah argued with God, wished himself dead, and accused God of being an unreliable liar (15:18).

Through this relationship and Jeremiah's doubts, you get a real example of what it means to FOLLOW GOD NO MATTER WHAT! You also learn that NO ONE escapes suffering. But God makes you strong enough to endure it. Finally, through his book, you should see that even though nations ABANDON GOD, GOD DOES NOT ABANDON THEM! He shows His powers each time anyone calls on Him.

LAMENTATIONS

The theme of the book of Lamentations is **TEARS**. This book consists of five poems of sorrow for the fallen city of Jerusalem, written by Jeremiah, as he witnessed everything that he described. The sadness was that disaster did not have to occur. Such is precisely the case today. You are warned to turn against your wicked ways. Yet, you don't take heed until it's too late.

These poems also teach you that when you reject God, He gets angry, and you get punished. Yet, there is hope, because when sin is eliminated, God forgives you and heals you. Tears are a necessary part of healing, and joy always follows tears.

EZEKIEL

To be truly alive, you must have the Spirit of God in you. If you don't have the Spirit of God, you're physically alive, but you're spiritually dead. In light of this, the theme of the book of Ezekiel is **DRY BONES** (chapter 37).

The book of Ezekiel is divided into three parts. In the first part, God promises the destruction of Jerusalem. Then, God predicted the downfall of Israel's neighbors. Finally, God promised a brighter future, because He didn't want to remain unclear and far away from His people. God wanted to live with His people, and make their city His home. Through all of these prophesies, the consistent message, is that God judges sin but remains faithful to His people. As such, how you live determines how God treats you. If you ignore God, you suffer until He gets your attention.

Despite the wicked tendencies of the nation back in the sixth century, and the wickedness of today, the book of Ezekiel clearly teaches that God is full of compassion, and He really doesn't want anyone to die and go to hell (34:11). As such, the million dollar question is, "Will you welcome the Spirit of God or will you remain as 'dry bones'?'"

DANIEL

As Daniel delivered many messages from God by interpreting dreams, the theme of the book of Daniel is **DREAMS**. One of the valuable lessons you learn from Daniel is how to live with and serve authority figures who do not share or respect your beliefs. Daniel had an unshakeable trust in God. As a result, he was exposed to barbaric persecution, including being thrown in a den of lions (chapter 6). Yet, even in this severe persecution, Daniel remained unharmed because he had the protection of God (6:22-23). From this, you see that God is the King of Kings, and He has the final say in the affairs of men.

As you read this short book, look for these several points:

(1:18-19) Godly wisdom and kowledge is superior.

(2:20-23) God answers ALL prayers IF you have faith, a humble spirit of obedience, praise, and thanksgiving.

(5:20-25) Your position should never allow you to forget the King of Kings.

(6:10-11) Trust God no matter what, because with Him, nothing is impossible.

(10:12-19) There's power in prayers. However, when prayers go unanswered for long periods, more work may be involved than you can ever imagine.

HOSEA

The theme of the book of Hosea is **HARLOT**. Hosea is a prophet who's married to a woman that turns to prostitution, in spite of her having his love, a home, his name, and a good reputation. Hosea's unhappy homelife symbolizes how Israel left God to seek after false gods. Just as Hosea continued to love his wife, God continues to love Israel and promises to one day restore the nation.

Harlot is the theme because whoredom and adultery of God's

people is presented. For example, Israel had no desire to please God. They had no faith; and they were rebellious and full of sin. Yet, God remained faithful, caring, forgiving, and kind.

This book first describes Hosea's tragic homelife; then Israel's rebellion against God; judgment to come; and promised restoration. Through this husband and wife analogy, you should see that God wants to be MORE than just your master (2:16). He wants to be like a husband. As such, your sins don't just break God's laws. They also break His heart.

JOEL

The theme of the book of Joel is **LOCUSTS**. Joel used the plague of this insect to warn Jerusalem about the coming judgment of God. Unlike other prophets who got consumed with emotions, Joel concentrated on solutions. For example, (1:13-14) Joel urged the priests to call for a nationwide day of prayer and fasting to lead the people back to God.

Since locusts destroy crops, which would eventually lead to the disappearance of food, and cause everyone to die of starvation, people had no where to turn, but to God. Sin is like locusts! It just multiplies and destroys everything it gets a hold of, and the only way to escape sin is through Jesus Christ.

AMOS

The theme of the book of Amos is **PLUMBLINE and OLIVE**. Amos, a farmer and a prophet, placed emphasis on injustice, including oppression of the poor (8:4-7), dishonesty in business, and bribery. The point is that God is righteous and He expects the same of you.

OBADIAH

The theme of the book of Obadiah is **BROTHER'S KEEPER**. Obadiah spoke about a feud between two brothers, Esau and Jacob. The violence between the two brothers passed from one generation to another, all because Esau was selfish and cared more about a meal than his family's name. His descendants cared more for a profit than for compassion towards a brother.

The underlying message that you should get from this 1-chapter book is God hates sin and He judges it accordingly.

JONAH

The theme of the book of Jonah is **FISH**. Jonah tells the story of a prophet whom God instructed to love his enemies in Nineveh. Jonah disobeyed by refusing to go to the people he hated. Jonah tried to runaway from God (1:3), but when he tried to escape by boat, he was thrown overboard and swallowed up by a great fish.

Jonah prayed to God from the inside of the fish, and God delivered him. Afterwards, Jonah preached in Nineveh as God instructed, and the entire city believed the message and repented (chapter 3). Thus, you should see that God loves ALL men, not just the Israelites or Christians. Just as He loves everyone, you must also love all people, and offer them salvation, as God does.

MICAH

The theme of the book of Micah is **DAY IN COURT**. Micah preaches to Israel and Judah, denouncing their idolatry and oppression (1:4-5), greed (2:2), and wickedness. God expects righteousness, justice, humility, and love, and not merely outward signs (6:6-12). When you fall short, you get judged. Still, God patiently waits for your repentance because He delights in forgiving and showing mercy.

NAHUM

The theme of the book of Nahum is **FLOOD**, and the overall message is that God is the power of all powers. The prophet, Nahum makes four points to convey this message. First, the causes for Nineveh's destruction was idolatry, murder, and superstition. Second, the city of Nineveh couldn't be tolerated because of the holiness of God. Third, anyone who trangresses God's laws are doomed to destruction. Finally, there's hope because God is slow to anger, and offers blessings to those who repent.

HABAKKUK

Today, whether you look at the corruption of the world, or the trials of your own life, you may wonder if God has lost control. God's power is NOT always visible, on the surface. However, a person of faith KNOWS God is behind everything. In light of this, the theme of the book of Habakkuk is **watchtower**.

Unlike other prophets who received messages from God and delivered them, Habakkuk questioned God, and climbed to his watchtower to wait for God's answers (2:1). Habakkuk wanted to know why God allowed evil to exist; and how could God use a sinful nation to punish another nation for its sins. God's reply was that the righteous must patiently wait and trust God in hard times.

ZEPHANIAH

The theme of the book of Zephaniah is **DAY OF THE LORD**. Judgment Day is coming and everyone should repent and get ready. Zephaniah described Judgment Day as a "supernatural event" involving God cleaning the whole world. This cleaning involved the removal of HYPOCRITES (1:5) who worshipped God and Malcham; BACK-

SLIDERS (1:6) who turned their backs on the Lord; and REBELS who never loved or wanted to love God.

As Zephaniah warns "prideful Jerusalem," chapter 3 teaches you the problem with being prideful. No one can tell you anything. You refuse all correction---even from God himself. You don't listen to the voice of God because you think you know just as much as God.

HAGGAI

The theme of the book of Haggai is **TEMPLE**. The book opens with the prophet, Haggai rebuking Judah for neglecting the temple. People got consumed with their own affairs and stopped working on the rebuilding of the temple. However, the temple was a place of worship and a necessity.

The underlying message of this book is that God SHOULD be first priority in your life, and when He's NOT, nothing else will truly succeed. This message is apparent today, when you reflect on people who spend 25 to 30 years or more of their life working, and they have little or nothing to show for it. Yet, when God is first, you don't have to work countless hours to keep from starving. God guides your daily activities. He leads you to prosperity. He teaches you how to manage your wealth. In short, all you can do is succeed, because God promises to bless you when He's first.

ZECHARIAH

The theme of the book of Zechariah is **MESSIAH**. Zechariah was a prophet sent by God to encourage everyone to return to the Lord and repent. Zechariah illustrates the power of God through (8) visions, but the vision prophesying the coming of Jesus Christ is the most important.

Repentance was a main subject of this book, because the Jews were partaking in fasting and other religious ceremonies, but there was no obedience to God. There was no heeding to previous warnings by other prophets. Because of these weaknesses (of religion without an intimate relationship with God), God made an allowance, by sending the Messiah.

This book should also teach you that God provides for ALL of your needs. He gives you protection, prosperity, strength, and grace. And since your greatest need is to know God intimately, He even offers you a Messiah to meet this need. If you feel defeated, it's NOT because God has forgotten you. It's because you are rejecting what God has made readily available to you. Thus, you must ask yourself why you are refusing God's blessings.

MALACHI

The theme of the book of Malachi is **HEARTS OF STONE**. As

Malachi describes the depth's of God's continuous love for His people, and how His people rejected His love, you see that God's people's hearts are in fact, hardened as stone. This book is one of the saddest books of the Bible! You see the corruption of priests, who are held most accountable for their sins, because they are SUPPOSE to KNOW the MOST. They're in a position to teach people God's laws. Yet, they lie, cheat, lust, steal, and offend God in other ways.

As you draw to the close of the Old Testament and hear from the last prophet of the era, ask yourself if your heart has hardened like stone? Are you able to continuously offend God with your sins and have no remorse? If so, look to the hope offered in the New Testament.

CHAPTER 7

FROM THE OLD TO THE NEW

I mentioned earlier that Satan uses tactics such as fear, racism, and education to keep people away from the Word of God. But Satan also fools people into thinking that they just don't have 15-30 minutes in a day, to give to God! Furthermore, the Bible has over 1,000 pages, and many people look at the size of the print, and the number of pages, and conclude that it's impossible to read the Bible from cover-to-cover! However, the Bible is very strategically laid out, and not nearly as confusing or complex as it seems.

The first book of the Bible gives you creation of the universe. But the first five books of the Bible also tells the origin and history of the Jews. The next twelve books, from Joshua to Esther gives you additional history. Then Job, Psalms, Proverbs, Ecclesiastes, and the Song of Solomon are books of poetry. Finally, the Old Testament closes after messages from (16) different prophets. The New Testament begins with (4) accounts of the life of Jesus Christ. The book of Acts tells what happened to Jesus' followers AFTER He left them. As two of Christ's Apostles became famous leaders, the remainder of the Bible deals with the Apostle's instructions for daily living. For example, Paul's (13) letters follow the book of Acts, and the remaining (9) letters conclude the Bible.

THE GOSPELS

The Old Testament shows you a corrupt world lost in sin. And God, being full of lovingkindness and mercy, promised the Jews, the Gentiles, and ultimately all the world, A Messiah to save them. God SAID that He would be born to a virgin, and IT WAS DONE! The Gospels according to Matthew, Mark, Luke, and John gives four accounts of Jesus Christ fulfilling God's promises made in the Old Testament. Thus, these four books tell you about the birth of Jesus; the life He led; His teachings; crucifixion and His resurrection.

The book of Matthew begins with the genealogy of Jesus Christ, tracing back to the descendants of Abraham and King David to show you that Jesus was a Jew. Jesus Christ was born to a virgin, named Mary, who was impregnated by the Holy Spirit. Jesus was born in Bethlehem, but brought to Nazareth, Israel, to escape orders that every baby boy under the age of 2 be killed.

While Jesus was in Nazareth, He was baptised by John the Baptist. This baptism of Christ showed how He humbled himself to a man. Then Jesus was led into the wilderness by the Holy Spirit. In the wilderness, Christ was tempted by Satan several times. When Satan realized he couldn't get Christ to give in to temptation, he left Him alone. Christ' resisting temptation showed that man can also resist the temptations of sin.

Valuable lessons that Christ teach, through the (4) Gospels include:

1) Godliness begins in the heart. If your heart is not kind, merciful, humble, and righteous, all the "ACTS" of kindness in the world will NOT get you into heaven. In addition, sin starts in the heart.

2) Godliness includes loving your enemy. God is not bias. He gives sunshine and rain to good and evil people.

3) Godliness does not allow for selfishness. Contrary to what you may THINK, Matthew 5:42 teaches you to give or loan if you are asked. You are not godly, if you see a poor person in need, and you're able to help them, but you don't.

4) God keeps His promises, so you should NEVER WORRY about obtaining food, or shelter, because God promises to take care of your basic needs. It is also unnecessary to work excessively, neglecting your rest, for the sake of "security."

5) Actions speak louder than words. Everyone who "sounds" religious is NOT godly.

6) No man can go to God, accept through His Son, Jesus Christ. Christ is the authority because NO OTHER has sacrificed their life for the sake of other's salvation. In order to exercise Christ's authority and receive the power of God, you must have faith in Him.

7) If you are one of God's Chosen Ones, Jesus teaches you to go to God's "lost sheep" and share the Good News, that Jesus lives.

8) Keep open arms to godly men.

9) ANY sin can be forgiven EXCEPT the one that speaks against the Holy Spirit (Matthew 12:31-32). It is the Holy Spirit that convicts you of your sins, and brings you to repentance. Without the Holy Spirit, you will be in bondage to sin.

10) An evil heart is what causes murder, adultery, stealing, lying, cheating, and fornication. Therefore, an evil heart is what defiles man, and NOTHING ELSE. Foods pass through your digestive system and out again. Food will not defile a man.

11) Miracles don't win souls. During Jesus' life, He healed multitudes of sick people, and performed one miracle after another. Yet, the miracles NEVER increased man's faith. They fascinated the crowds. But shortly after, the miracles were forgotten.

12) Salvation is for EVERYONE! But some people will hear the Good News and not understand it. Satan will then come and snatch away the TRUTH that was put in their heart. Others will hear the TRUTH, receive it with real joy, but since they have no depth in their life, the seeds of truth don't root very deeply. As a result, when trouble comes, enthusiasm fades, and they turn their back on the truth. Some people will hear the truth, but the cares of this life, and the longing for money will drown out God's Word. Then they'll do less and less for God. Finally, there are some people who will listen to the truth; understand it; and go out and share this Good News, pointing 30 to 100 or more souls to Christ. Which of these persons describe you?

13) There is but ONE Father, One Master, and One Rabbi. He is God, our Creator. Therefore, you should call no one on earth, "Father," "Master," or "Rabbi." Everyone is your brother or sister.

14) Call on the name of Jesus, because He understands. Jesus has needs just like us. He needed food and friends. He got lonely and tired, and He sowed anger and disappointment. So, He understands us perfectly. He was always teaching. But He enjoyed His quiet time, and He liked His boat.

15) Jesus Christ did not die so that we could live in poverty until we die and go to heaven. However, you also were not put here to get rich and forget your King either. Jesus warns you NOT to put your faith in your money, because money serves no purpose on your death bed.

16) God and Jesus are separate bodies. Yet, they are one, as in a marriage. If you accept Christ as your Personal Savior, you marry God and Jesus. You become 3 as 1. The marriage forms the Trinity.

THE BOOK OF ACTS
The book of Acts teaches you that what Jesus started on earth, He continued through the churches. Thus, you see the life of the church, the spread of the Gospel from Jews to Gentiles, activities of the apostle Peter, and persecution of believers. Important lessons that come through this book are as follows:
1) It takes courage and obedience to live by faith.

2) A good church is filled with the Holy Spirit; there's proper teaching and praying; warm fellowship among its believers; no poverty; and healing.

3) As you deliver the truth, REMEMBER that the world persecuted Jesus Christ and didn't listen to Him! You are no better. You will also

be persecuted and ignored. You can't save the world. When you deliver the truth and leave the rest to God, people have no excuse for sinning, and you have been set free of your responsibility, by giving the truth.

4) Why did the Jews hate Jesus Christ? Christ was a healer, a teacher, and He performed miracles. Yet the Jews expected more! The Jews expected a king on a white horse, and they got a plainly dressed Messiah on a donkey. Their worldly expectations were not met.

5) Many people don't go to church because they don't feel "good" enough. They don't have the "nerves" to step in a church. However, you do NOT have to have a pure heart in order to go to God for salvation. God wants you to come just as you are. Churches are like hospitals. They're for "sick" people. If you're addicted to drugs, alcohol, or whatever, there's NO BETTER PLACE for you to be than church.

WHAT ARE SOME OF THE MOST IMPORTANT MESSAGES OF THE APOSTLE PAUL'S (13) LETTERS?

1) Many people know of God's existence, but they won't admit it, worship Him, or thank Him for His daily care. Instead, people make their own rules, wander in darkness, and make money and sex their gods. However, when the Holy Spirit delivers you from despair, you should share this joy with the world.

2) According to Romans 2:12-15, salvation is NOT given to those who KNOW what to do, unless they do it. Saints cannot accept Jesus Christ as Lord and continue to live as if they NEVER got saved. 2:25 points to the fallacy of man who gains knowledge of the Bible, and becomes proud of knowing God's laws, but dishonors God by breaking His laws.

3) Salvation is a free gift. You do not earn it by being good. God declares sinners good if they have faith in Jesus, to save them from the wrath. However, your actions determine where your heart is and whether or not you really have faith. You are truly a servant to whom ever you obey.

4) What comes after faith?
    a. You have peace with God because you've been made right, in His eyes by faith.
    b. God brings you into highest privilege, where you look forward to becoming ALL that God has in mind for you to be.
    c. You rejoice when faced with problems because you KNOW they

are for your good. You learn patience.

d. You stand firmly no matter what because you know how much God deeply loves you.

e. You feel God's warm love within, because He's given you the Holy Spirit to fill your heart with His love (Romans 5:5)

f. You get to pray, grow, bless, and be more abundantly blessed. You get to enjoy life serving your Friend, Jesus Christ.

5) Romans chapter 8 teaches that obedience to the Holy Spirit is a requirement for eternal life, as well as faith in Jesus Christ.

6) Theology is worthless unless it makes a difference in how you live. Christians should:

a. Remember they are all parts of the body of Christ, and therefore need each other.

b. Take responsibilities seriously.

c. Serve the Lord enthusiastically.

d. Be prayerful and patient in times of trouble.

e. Help God's children in need.

f. Pray for those who persecute you.

g. Habitually invite guests home for dinner.

h. Don't think you know it all.

i. Don't quarrel

j. Obey the law and pay your taxes.

k. Don't spend your time in wild parties, getting drunk, or in adultery and lust.

l. Ask Jesus to help you live as you should.

m. Be considerate of other people's feelings, and strive to please others, NOT yourself.

n. Pray for each other and refresh each other.

o. Never engage in religious debates. Whether you eat meat or not is between you and God. God has the power to make people change as they should. Regarding holiday celebrations, everyone should decide for himself. What's most important is that you strive for goodness and flee evil.

1 CORINTHIANS

Paul's second letter was addressed to a church he established in Corinth. This letter was written because several years after Paul left, problems arose among the church. The Corinthians worshipped money and all the exotic things it could buy. Key messages were as follows:

1) There should be harmony in the church. Division comes about when there is inadequate or improper teaching, and everyone is NOT on the same wave-lengths, which should be Jesus Christ.

2) You should separate from Christians who engage in sexual sin, greed, and abusiveness, because sin is cancerous and it spreads. If you tolerate sin in the church, everyone will be affected.

3) Anyone can fall into sin. But NO temptation is irresistable. You just need to trust God To protect you from temptation.

4) To believe in the Good News, you must believe that dead people come back to life through resurrection. If you don't believe this, then:
a. Jesus is still dead.

b. Baptism is pointless.

c. All Apostles are "useless liars" because they ALL SAID THAT GOD RAISED JESUS FROM THE DEAD. Yet, this is NOT true if Jesus is still dead.

d. Your trust in God is EMPTY, WORTHLESS, and HOPELESS, and it's foolish to keep on trusting Him to save you, because you're under condemnation for your sins.

e. You should just "eat, drink, and be merry," because when you die, that's it. In TRUTH, there were many eye-witnesses to Christ's death and resurrection. For example, Christ was seen by Peter, then the "12", then five hundred Christian brothers at one time.

2 CORINTHIANS

The most important points Paul make in the book of 2 Corinthians is:

1) Ministers must be careful to NOT teach others that they must obey God's laws or die and go to hell. The old system required you to keep the Ten Commandments or face being stoned to death. Under the new system, you must allow the Holy Spirit to give you life. This false teaching discourages many people from even going to church. They know that they've broken the Ten Commandments, so they think they're doomed and, "why bother?" The truth properly taught would free many people from a sense of hopelessness.

2) It's a blessing when God chooses you to tell His Good News to others. The rules you must follow are:

   a. Never trick people into believing the Truth.

   b. Keep it simple! God's Word is NOT complicated.

   c. Give the Good News boldly.

GALATIANS

The main theme of this letter is that you are saved by the grace of God, through faith in Jesus Christ, and NOTHING else! Paul teaches that ANYTHING other than this is a perversion of the truth. Your salvation, however, does involve submission to the Spirit of God (5:16). In addition, there is nothing you can do to make God love you more or less. God loves you, and He never changes, so you don't have to earn His love, by trying to follow rules.

EPHESIANS

If you feel discouraged or wonder if God really cares, or if you question whether Christian life is worth the effort, read Ephesians! Paul wrote this letter to comfort and encourage believers in Ephesius.

One of the key points in this letter is that ALL of your battles in life are spiritual. So you should use ALL of God's armor to fight the enemy when he attacks:

a. A strong belt of Truth.

b. Breastplate of God's Approval (A righteous heart).

c. Shoes that speed you on as you preach the Good News of Peace with God.

d. A shield of faith.

e. Helmet of Salvation.

f. Sword of the Spirit, (Word of God).

g. Pray all the time.

PHILIPPIANS

Paul's letter to the Philippians was a thank you note, expressing his appreciation for their friendship. This letter gives one basic message. In all things, REJOICE. Even if you're facing death, rejoice. The message did not mean that Christians wouldn't face problems. Even Jesus Christ had to endure the cross. Yet, it was for the good of all mankind.

Paul didn't just encourage others to rejoice. He knew how to be content in every situation, be it wealth or poverty, a full stomach or hunger. Thus, Paul teaches you to experience God's peace; and don't worry about anything. God's peace will keep your thoughts and heart quiet and at rest, as you trust Jesus Christ.

COLOSSIANS

Colosse was located on a major trade route from the East, and had heavy dealings with Oriental traders with mysterious religions. As a result, Colosse was a prime area for the growth of cults. Paul, therefore, addressed this letter to the Colossians. The important points he made in this letter were:

1.) Jesus Christ is all-sufficient, so trust Him for your daily concerns. You don't need cults or astrology, or witchcraft.

2.) Don't let others spoil your faith and joy, with their philosophies, instead of what Jesus said.

3.) Don't let others criticize you for what you eat or drink, or for not celebrating Jewish holidays, feasts, ceremonies, or Sabbaths.

1 THESSALONIANS

Paul wrote this letter to comfort and encourage persecuted believers. He encouraged them to stand firm and continue to live godly lives even under persecution, because God promised you the ultimate victory to occur at the return of Christ. Paul reminds you that God punishes those who hinder or persecute His messengers. Also, Paul reminds you that hard times are suppose to make you grow stronger in the Lord.

2 THESSALONIANS

In this letter, Paul assures believers that Christ will return, because God ALWAYS has victory over evil. Other points Paul make in this short letter are:

1.) You have a duty to thank God for using you to increase other's faith, and increase love between each other.

2.) Pray that God uses you entirely for His purpose.

3.) Pray for protection from evil men, because NOT everyone loves the Lord.

4.) Avoid Christians who are lazy and don't follow the ideal of hard work (3:1-15). Don't think of lazy people as an enemy. Just warn them as a brother or sister.

5.) In the end of time, two things are going to happen:
a. There will be great rebellion against God

b. The son of hell will come and defy every good, then destroy every other object of adoration and worship. He will pretend to be God. Everyone on their way to hell because they rejected the truth, will be fooled.

1 TIMOTHY
Paul wrote a letter to Timothy to address problems in the church, so that churches would function properly. The major theme of the letter was that there be consistency between the correct Christian doctrine and the proper Christian behavior. For example, churches must refrain from personal opinions, and Christians must make a point of living godly lives as they are taught. Other points brought out include:
1.) Since pastors have the difficult position of being a social worker, hospital chaplain, administrator, teacher, personnel director, and communicator, you should show greater compassion for them.

2.) Both prisons and churches are filled with very sick people, and 1:12-16 shows that the sicker you are, the more God wants to work on you and win you over.

3.) Although false teachers speak against eating certain foods, EVERYTHING that God created is good and for your enjoyment. So, if you are thankful, and ask God to bless your food, it will be made good by the Word of God and prayer.

2 TIMOTHY
Paul wrote this letter near the end of his life, to encourage Timothy to stand firm in the face of persecution. Because God has sovereign control over everything, you CAN TRUST HIM, and fear is not necessary. This letter, written to encourage Christian workers

made several other key points:

1.) ALL Scriptures is inspired by God, and is beneficial for doctrine, correction, and instruction on righteous living (3:16).

2.) God's people should NOT be quarrelsome. They should be gentle, patient, and humble, when trying to teach someone mixed up about the truth. They are more likely to get positive results.

TITUS

This letter, addressed to Paul's associate, Titus, stresses the importance of proper Christian living in the midst of a hostile and corrupt world. This letter also teaches that you can identify a false teacher, by the words he speak. For example, a person with a pure heart sees goodness in everything. But a person with an evil heart is untrusting, and finds evil in everything. He has a dirty mind, a rebellious heart, and claims to know God, but his actions say he don't.

PHILEMON

Onesimus was a slave, and Philemon was a slave owner, and the two became Christian brothers because of a letter Paul had written to Philemon. Paul's letter started off with gentleness, truth, and some flattery, and led to a godly request for Philemon to be kind to a child of God who just happened to be his runaway slave.

The very significant messages that come from this very short letter are:

1.) No one, not even a runaway slave, is beyond the Word of God.

2.) Anyone who trusts Jesus Christ will become new and receive the blessings God promised.

3.) God's Word is powerful enough to break down an entire evil system of slavery, through Christian teaching.

4.) God is faithful, and this will become even more apparent when He does away with all evil in the end of time.

OTHER LETTERS

HEBREWS

The book of Hebrews teaches you:

1.) Jesus Christ is superior to every other religious system.

2.) Angels are spirit-messengers sent out to help God's Chosen ones, but Christ's death and resurrection for man makes Him superior to angels. No one else has sacrificed their life for the sake of sending multitudes of God's people to heaven.

3.) **Regarding Faith:**
a. It's impossible to please God without it.

b. Great promises await those who keep the faith.

c. Your character is strengthened by faith.

d. You cannot know the truth about forgiveness, and purposely sin, by rejecting the Holy Spirit. Christ's death does NOT cover this sin.

4.) **How do you keep the faith?**
a. Eliminate anything that slows you down or holds you back.

b. Run patiently.

c. Let Christ lead and instruct you. Stay prayerful.

d. If you grow weary, remember Christ as He patiently let men torment Him.

e. Remember all suffering brings about a lesson to be learned, and learning brings about growth.

f. Remember you're a child of God and God loves you. True love is longsuffering, as well as faithful.

g. Stay peaceful and holy.

JAMES
The book of James was written to show that faith without actions is nothing. Saying you have faith is NOT enough. The Gospels change lives, and if you commit yourself to Christ, your faith will generate acts of love and kindness. ACTIONS do NOT CAUSE life. They simply PROVE THAT LIFE IS PRESENT. Moreover, true religious conduct teaches:
1.) It's better to listen a lot, speak a little, and not get angry.

2.) If you don't act on the Word, you'll forget it.

3.) Christians must control their tongues. If you control your tongue, you'll have control in every other area of your life.

4.) Wisdom from God is full of quiet gentleness, and it makes you peaceful, and willing to surrender to others and allow for discussion.

1 PETER

1 Peter was originally written to people in severe danger, but since EVERYONE experiences suffering, the messages apply to all of us:

1.) When you suffer, sin loses its power and you don't spend the rest of your life chasing evil desires.

2.) All Christians will be tested by fire (1:7). Fire melts off all impurities, and brings about true, purified gold. Suffering exposes your true level of faith and refines it. Faith in the midst of trials results in rewards.

2 PETER

2 Peter encourages you to grow spiritually despite false teachers lifting up their own ideas about what is truth. You should remain steadfast because the world is trying to undo the work of God.

1.) You can resist temptation by:

a. living godly, including forsaking your own desires and doing what you know is right.

b. believing the truth

c. enduring persecution

d. trusting God

e. anticipating Christ's return.

2.) Remember that NO Scripture was ever thought up by the prophet himself. The Holy Spirit, in these prophets, gave messages from God.

3.) Christ is going to return, but God is giving us time to get His message of salvation out to others.

4.) Be weary of people who are "deliberately stupid," always demanding unusual interpretations (3:16). If you're not careful, you will also become mixed up and confused.

1 JOHN

1 John stresses basic truths of Chrisitianity regarding love, faith, and righteousness. Significant points made in this letter include:

1.) **(2:22-23) "THE GREATEST LIAR IS the one who says Jesus is NOT Christ. This is an antichrist, and a person who doesn't believe in Christ, God's Son, can't have God, the Father either. But he who has Christ, God's Son, has God the Father also!"**

2.) Stay away from anything that can take God's place in your heart.

3.) If you say you have no sins, you are a liar, and you're calling God a liar. Every man sins. You must confess your sins to God and ask for forgiveness and cleansing.

4.) ARE YOU REALLY TRYING TO DO WHAT GOD WANTS YOU TO DO? If the answer is yes, you belong to Christ.

2 JOHN

The main idea of this short book is to remind Christians of the existence of false doctrine. False teachers don't believe that Jesus Christ came to earth as a human being with a body like ours. 2 John also reminds you that to love God is to obey Him.

3 JOHN

This letter encourages John's friend Gaius to support an evangelist who's preaching the truth. The underlying message is that Christians should support one another in the works of God. Otherwise, you are supporting Satan, who's main objective is to destroy believers. On the other hand, Christians must use discretion, because of false teachers who don't teach the truth about Christ.

JUDE

The book of Jude teaches you that:
1.) You should defend the truth.

2.) Avoid selfishness, greed, and rebelliousness.

REVELATIONS

The book of Revelations is packed with symbolism. Some people get utterly confused as they read this book. Others read it and come up with their own interpretation. Don't panic as you step into the last book of the Bible. Just read the symbols and ask, "What does this tell me about Jesus Christ, God, history, or the future?" Don't analyze these details as you read. In the end, what you should get, after reading this book, is a concise picture of Christ Jesus, as a mighty ruler!

In the book of Revelations, God allowed Jesus Christ to reveal the future to John in visions. An angel was sent from heaven to explain the visions, and John simply recorded everything he saw and heard. **One of John's visions** consisted of Jesus Christ wearing a long robe with a golden band across His chest, and holding seven gold candlesticks and seven stars. Then John got messages from seven letters addressed to churches in Ephesus, Smyrna, Pergamos, Thyatira, Sardis, Philadelphia, and Laodicea. **John then sees** (4) beasts---an eagle, bull, lion, and man, and questions their worthiness to open the Book of History. Twenty-four elders surrounding the throne of Jesus

Christ are seen in a vision.

The significance of these visions is that Christ alone is worthy to be praised. An additional vision of the Lamb and the Book of Life again raised the question, "Who in all the world is worthy to break the seven seals on the Book of Life? Millions of angels, the four beasts, and the twenty-four elders ALL agreed that the Little slain Lamb alone, was worthy of all, to unseal and open the Book of Life.

This wonderful little Lamb was Jesus Christ. No one has ever had that magnitude of love that said, "Father, they are ALL sinners, but don't cast them all to hell. Have mercy on them. Take my life and let me pray for their sins with my blood. If they repent or be truly sorry for their sins, and accept me as their Savior, Father, free these men and make them your children." This magnitude of love made Christ the Lamb worthy of Power, Wisdom, Strength, Honor, Glory, and Blessing.

On this note, if you're going through a broken marriage, battling drugs or alcohol, you're tired of suffering, and you feel like you just want to give up---VISUALIZE THE LITTLE WOUNDED LAMB who appeared in John's vision. Remember that this little innocent, precious Lamb was slain so that you wouldn't have to suffer in darkness. Embrace this precious little Lamb and feel His love, strength, power, and glory. Jesus lives!

The other remaining visions describe the death and destruction that's to come to all those who rejected the little slain Lamb. The end of Revelations shows brightness of our future. You read about a New Jerusalem paved with gold, and gates made with pearls, and ultimately, EVIL PUT TO REST. Thus, the future is bright indeed!

CONCLUSION

I've exhausted myself with words, and I believe I've built a case, and given you adequate information for YOU to decide whether or not you'll heed my advice. So my closing remarks are that the Word of God is a delight, and it was a sheer pleasure sharing my wealth with you.

May God bless you with some fresh milk and honey, and a comfortable, cozy chair as you feast on His Word! I welcome your prayer requests, comments, questions, and other concerns or for additional copies write to:
c/o Pamela M. Harris
4004 Arborwood
Lindenwold, NJ 08021

APPENDIX

ADDITIONAL REFERENCES

Books.

A Concise Dictionary of Cults and Religions, by William Watson.

A Handbook of Living Religions, edited by John R. Hinnells, c.1984.

Christianity and the World Religions, Paths to Dialogue with Islam, Hinduism, and Buddhism, by Hans Hung, Josef Van Ess, Heinrich Von Stietencion

The Bible in the Making, by Geddes MacGregor, J.B. Lippincott Company, Philadelphia and New York, c. 1959.

World in View Israel, by Mike Rogoff, c.1991.

VIDEOS.

New Age Bible Versions, by G. A. Riplinger. (Can be ordered by Wards Christian Bookstore, Burlington, New Jersey 08016).

BOOKS OF THE BIBLE

BOOK	CHAPTERS	BOOK	CHAPTER
Genesis	50	Micah	7
Exodus	40	Nahum	3
Leviticus	27	Habakkuk	3
Numbers	36	Zephaniah	3
Deuteronomy	34	Haggai	2
Joshua	24	Zechariah	14
Judges	21	Malachi	4
Ruth	4		
1 Samuel	31	Matthew	28
2 Samuel	24	Mark	16
1 Kings	22	Luke	24
2 Kings	25	John	21
1 Chronicles	29		
2 Chronicles	36	Acts	28
Ezra	10		
Nehemiah	13	Romans	16
Esther	10	1 Corinthians	16
		2 Corinthians	13
Job	42	Galatians	6
Psalms	150	Ephesians	6
Proverbs	31	Philippians	4
Ecclesiastes	12	Colossians	4
Song of Solomon	8	1 Thessalonians	5
		2 Thessalonians	3
Isaiah	66	1 Timothy	6
Jeremiah	5	2 Timothy	4
Lamentations	5	Titus	3
Ezekiel	48	Philemon	1
Daniel	12		
Hosea	14	Hebrews	13
Joel	3	James	5
Amos	9	1 Peter	5
Obadiah	1	2 Peter	3
Jonah	4	1, 2, 3, John	1
		Jude	1
		Revelations	22

READ THE BIBLE IN ONE YEAR

January

01	Genesis 1-4
02	Genesis 5-7
03	Genesis 8-9
04	Genesis 10-13
05	Genesis 14-15
06	Genesis 16-17
07	Genesis 18-19
08	Genesis 20-21
09	Genesis 22-24
10	Genesis 25-28
11	Genesis 29-30
12	Genesis 31-32
13	Genesis 33-34
14	Genesis 35-36
15	Genesis 37-40
16	Genesis 41-42
17	Genesis 43-44
18	Genesis 45-46
19	Genesis 47-48
20	Genesis 49-50
21	Exodus 1-4
22	Exodus 5-6
23	Exodus 7-8
24	Exodus 9-10
25	Exodus 11-12
26	Exodus 13-16
27	Exodus 17-20
28	Exodus 21-22
29	Exodus 23-26
30	Exodus 27-28
31	Exodus 29-30

February

01	Exodus 31-34
02	Exodus 35-36
03	Exodus 37-38
04	Exodus 39-40
05	Leviticus 1-2
06	Leviticus 3-4
07	Leviticus 5-8
08	Leviticus 9-12
09	Leviticus 13
10	Leviticus 14
11	Leviticus 15-18
12	Leviticus 19-22
13	Leviticus 23-25
14	Leviticus 26-27
15	Numbers 1-2
16	Numbers 3-4
17	Numbers 5-7
18	Numbers 8-11
19	Numbers 12-13
20	Numbers 14-16
21	Numbers 17-18
22	Numbers 19-20
23	Numbers 21-24
24	Numbers 25-26
25	Numbers 27-30
26	Numbers 31-34
27	Numbers 35-36
28	Deuteronomy 1-2

READ THE BIBLE IN ONE YEAR

March		**April**	
01	Deuteronomy 3-6	01	1 Samuel 11-13
02	Deuteronomy 7-10	02	1 Samuel 14-15
03	Deuteronomy 11-12	03	1 Samuel 16-17
04	Deuteronomy 13-16	04	1 Samuel 18-20
05	Deuteronomy 17-20	05	1 Samuel 21-24
06	Deuteronomy 21-22	06	1 Samuel 25-27
07	Deuteronomy 23-24	07	1 Samuel 28-31
08	Deuteronomy 25-27	08	2 Samuel 1-3
09	Deuteronomy 28-31	09	2 Samuel 4-7
10	Deuteronomy 32	10	2 Samuel 8-11
11	Deuteronomy 33-34	11	2 Samuel 12-13
12	Joshua 1-4	12	2 Samuel 14-15
13	Joshua 5-6	13	2 Samuel 16-17
14	Joshua 7-8	14	2 Samuel 18-19
15	Joshua 9-12	15	2 Samuel 20-22
16	Joshua 13-16	16	2 Samuel 23-24
17	Joshua 17-20	17	1 Kings 1
18	Joshua 21-22	18	1 Kings 2-3
19	Joshua 23-24	19	1 Kings 4-6
20	Judges 1-3	20	1 Kings 7
21	Judges 4-6	21	1 Kings 8
22	Judges 7-8	22	1 Kings 9-10
23	Judges 9-10	23	1 Kings 11-12
24	Judges 11-13	24	1 Kings 13-14
25	Judges 14-16	25	1 Kings 15-17
26	Judges 17-19	26	1 Kings 18-19
27	Judges 20-21	27	1 Kings 20-21
28	Ruth 1-4	28	1 Kings 22; 2 Kings 1
29	1 Samuel 1-3	29	2 Kings 2-4
30	1 Samuel 4-7	30	2 Kings 5-7
31	1 Samuel 8-10		

READ THE BIBLE IN ONE YEAR

May

01	2 Kings 8-9
02	2 Kings 10-12
03	2 Kings 13-14
04	2 Kings 15-16
05	2 Kings 17-18
06	2 Kings 19-21
07	2 Kings 22-25
08	1 Chronicles 1
09	1 Chronicles 2-4
10	1 Chronicles 5-6
11	1 Chronicles 7-9
12	1 Chronicles 10-12
13	1 Chronicles 13-16
14	1 Chronicles 17-19
15	1 Chronicles 20-23
16	1 Chronicles 24-26
17	1 Chronicles 27-29
18	2 Chronicles 1-4
19	2 Chronicles 5-7
20	2 Chronicles 8-10
21	2 Chronicles 11-14
22	2 Chronicles 15-18
23	2 Chronicles 19-22
24	2 Chronicles 23-25
25	2 Chronicles 26-28
26	2 Chronicles 29-30
27	2 Chronicles 31-33
28	2 Chronicles 34-35
29	2 Chronicles 36; Ezra 1-2
30	Ezra 3-5
31	Ezra 6-8

June

01	Ezra 9-10
02	Nehemiah 1-3
03	Nehemiah 4-6
04	Nehemiah 7-8
05	Nehemiah 9-10
06	Nehemiah 11-13
07	Esther 1-3
08	Esther 4-7
09	Esther 8-10
10	Job 1-5
11	Job 6-10
12	Job 11-15
13	Job 16-21
14	Job 22-28
15	Job 29-33
16	Job 34-37
17	Job 38-42
18	Psalms 1-9
19	Psalms 10-17
20	Psalms 18-22
21	Psalms 23-31
22	Psalms 32-37
23	Psalms 38-44
24	Psalms 45-51
25	Psalms 52-59
26	Psalms 60-67
27	Psalms 68-71
28	Psalms 72-77
29	Psalms 78-81
30	Psalms 82-89

READ THE BIBLE IN ONE YEAR

July		August	
01	Psalms 90-97	01	Isaiah 43-47
02	Psalms 98-104	02	Isaiah 48-51
03	Psalms 105-107	03	Isaiah 52-56
04	Psalms 108-116	04	Isaiah 57-59
05	Psalms 117-119:72	05	Isaiah 60-63
06	Psalms 119:73-176	06	Isaiah 64-66
07	Psalms 120-135	07	Jeremiah 1-3
08	Psalms 136-142	08	Jeremiah 4-6
09	Psalms 143-150	09	Jeremiah 7-9
10	Proverbs 1-4	10	Jeremiah 10-12
11	Proverbs 5-8	11	Jeremiah 13-15
12	Proverbs 9-13	12	Jeremiah 16-18
13	Proverbs 14-17	13	Jeremiah 19-22
14	Proverbs 18-21	14	Jeremiah 23-25:16
15	Proverbs 22-24	15	Jeremiah 25:17-27
16	Proverbs 25-28	16	Jeremiah 28-30
17	Proverbs 29-31	17	Jeremiah 31-32
18	Ecclesiastes 1-6	18	Jeremiah 33-35
19	Ecclesiastes 7-12	19	Jeremiah 36-38
20	Song of Solomon 1-8	20	Jeremiah 39-41
21	Isaiah 1-4	21	Jeremiah 42-44
22	Isaiah 5-8	22	Jeremiah 45-48
23	Isaiah 9-12	23	Jeremiah 49-50
24	Isaiah 13-16	24	Jeremiah 51-52
25	Isaiah 17-21	25	Lamentations 1-2
26	Isaiah 22-25	26	Lamentations 3-5
27	Isaiah 26-28	27	Ezekiel 1-4
28	Isaiah 29-31	28	Ezekiel 5-8
29	Isaiah 32-35	29	Ezekiel 9-12
30	Isaiah 36-38	30	Ezekiel 13-15
31	Isaiah 39-42	31	Ezekiel 16

READ THE BIBLE IN ONE YEAR

September		October	
01	Ezekiel 17-19	01	Zechariah 11-14
02	Ezekiel 20-21	02	Malachi 1-4
03	Ezekiel 22-23	03	Matthew 1-4
04	Ezekiel 24-26	04	Matthew 5-6
05	Ezekiel 27-28	05	Matthew 7-9
06	Ezekiel 29-31	06	Matthew 10-12
07	Ezekiel 32-33	07	Matthew 13-14
08	Ezekiel 34-36	08	Matthew 15-17
09	Ezekiel 37-38	09	Matthew 18-20
10	Ezekiel 39-40	10	Matthew 21-22
11	Ezekiel 41-43	11	Matthew 23-24
12	Ezekiel 44-45	12	Matthew 25-26
13	Ezekiel 46-48	13	Matthew 27-28
14	Daniel 1-2	14	Mark 1-3
15	Daniel 3-4	15	Mark 4-5
16	Daniel 5-6	16	Mark 6-7
17	Daniel 7-8	17	Mark 8-9
18	Daniel 9-10	18	Mark 10-11
19	Daniel 11-12	19	Mark 12-13
20	Hosea 1-6	20	Mark 14-16
21	Hosea 7-12	21	Luke 1
22	Hosea 13-14; Joel	22	Luke 2-3
23	Amos 1-5	23	Luke 4-5
24	Amos 6-9; Obadiah	24	Luke 6-7
25	Jonah 1-4; Micah 1-2	25	Luke 8
26	Micah 3-7	26	Luke 9
27	Nahum; Habakkuk	27	Luke 10-11
28	Zephaniah; Haggai	28	Luke 12-13
29	Zechariah 1-6	29	Luke 14-16
30	Zechariah 7-10	30	Luke 17-18
		31	Luke 19-20

READ THE BIBLE IN ONE YEAR

November		December	
01	Luke 21-22	01	1 Corinthians 12-14
02	Luke 23-24	02	1 Corinthians 15-16
03	John 1-3	03	2 Corinthians 1-4
04	John 4-5	04	2 Corinthians 5-8
05	John 6-7	05	2 Corinthians 9-13
06	John 8-9	06	Galatians 1-4
07	John 10-11	07	Galatians 5-6; Ephesians 1-2
08	John 12-13	08	Ephesians 3-6
09	John 14-16	09	Philippians 1-4
10	John 17-18	10	Colossians 1-4
11	John 19-21	11	1 Thessalonians 1-4
12	Acts 1-3	12	1 Thess. 5; 2 Thess.1-3
13	Acts 4-6	13	1 Timothy 1-4
14	Acts 7-8	14	1 Timothy 5-6
15	Acts 9-10	15	2 Timothy 1-4
16	Acts 11-13	16	Titus 1-3; Philemon
17	Acts 14-16	17	Hebrews 1-5
18	Acts 17-18	18	Hebrews 6-9
19	Acts 19-20	19	Hebrews 10-11
20	Acts 21-22	20	Hebrews 12-13
21	Acts 23-25	21	James 1-5
22	Acts 26-28	22	1 Peter 1-4
23	Romans 1-3	23	1 Peter 5; 2 Peter 1-3
24	Romans 4-7	24	1 John 1-5
25	Romans 8-10	25	2 John; 3 John; Jude
26	Romans 11-14	26	Revelations 1-3
27	Romans 15-16	27	Revelations 4-8
28	1 Corinthians 1-4	28	Revelations 9-12
29	1 Corinthians 5-8	29	Revelations 13-16
30	1 Corinthians 9-11	30	Revelations 17-19
		31	Revelations 20-22